AUTHOR

Luigi Manes was born in Milan on July 18, 1966. He has a degree in Business Administration. Always interested in the history of the Second World War, in 2018 he published his first book, "Italy 43-45 – AFVs and MVs of co-belligerent units" (Mattioli 1885), together with Paolo Crippa, followed shortly after by "Carri armati Sherman in Sicilia" (Edizioni Ardite), written with Lorenzo Bovi. With Soldiershop he published "The Sherman medium tank in the European Theater of Operations" (2019), "British tracked carriers of World War Two" (2019), "Yugoslavian armored units 1940-45" (2020, this last book a four-handed work with Paolo Crippa), "The Legnano Combat Group" (2021), "Partisan Tanks" (2022, together with Paolo Crippa) and "Albanian units in the Second World War" (2023). He has written various articles for the military modeling magazine "Steel Art" and the website "Modellismo Più". Passionate about football, he is a great supporter of F.C. Internazionale Milano.

PUBLISHING'S NOTES

None of unpublished images or text of our book may be reproduced in any format without the expressed written permission of Luca Cristini Editore (already Soldiershop.com) when not indicate as marked with license creative commons 3.0 or 4.0. Luca Cristini Editore has made every reasonable effort to locate, contact and acknowledge rights holders and to correctly apply terms and conditions to Content.

Every effort has been made to trace the copyright of all the photographs. If there are unintentional omissions, please contact the publisher in writing at: info@soldiershop.com, who will correct all subsequent editions.

Our trademark: Luca Cristini Editore©, and the names of our series & brand: Soldiershop, Witness to war, Museum book, Bookmoon, Soldiers&Weapons, Battlefield, War in colour, Historical Biographies, Darwin's view, Fabula, Altrastoria, Italia Storica Ebook, Witness To History, Soldiers, Weapons & Uniforms, Storia etc. are herein © by Luca Cristini Editore.

LICENSES COMMONS

This book may utilize part of material marked with license creative commons 3.0 or 4.0 (CC BY 4.0), (CC BY-ND 4.0), (CC BY-SA 4.0) or (CC0 1.0). We give appropriate attribution credit and indicate if change were made in the acknowledgments field. Our WTW books series utilize only fonts licensed under the SIL Open Font License or other free use license.

For a complete list of Soldiershop titles please contact Luca Cristini Editore on our website: www.soldiershop.com or www.cristinieditore.com. E-mail: info@soldiershop.com

Titolo: **THE 28th GARIBALDI BRIGADE "MARIO GORDINI"** Code.: **WTW-066 EN**
By Luigi Manes
ISBN code: 979125589XXXX. First edition: April 2025.
Language: English; size: 177,8x254mm Cover & Art Design: Luca S. Cristini

WITNESS TO WAR (SOLDIERSHOP) is a trademark of Luca Cristini Editore, via Orio, 33D - 24050 Zanica (BG) ITALY.

WITNESS TO WAR

THE 28th GARIBALDI BRIGADE "MARIO GORDINI"

PHOTOS & IMAGES FROM WORLD WARTIME ARCHIVES

LUIGI MANES

BOOKS TO COLLECT

CONTENTS

Introduction..5

Formation and operations of the 28th GAP Brigade "Mario Gordini"...................7

The Liberation of Ravenna and the "Battle of the Valleys"...................................19

The 28th Garibaldi Brigade "Mario Gordini"...33

The "Mario Gordini" Brigade enters the front line...39

The "Mario Gordini" Brigade takes part in the final Allied offensive on the Italian front......65

End of operations and disbandment of the Brigade..75

Bibliography..98

INTRODUCTION

The 28th Garibaldi Brigade *"Mario Gordini"* was, together with the *"Modena"* Division and the *"Maiella"* Brigade, one of the great Resistance formations included in the Allied 15th Army Group during the Italian campaign. Although communist-inspired, this unit also counted in its ranks Actionists, Catholics, Republicans, Socialists and apolitical people.

Initially constituted as a GAP Brigade (Patriotic Action Groups), it was named after Mario Gordini, prominent figure of the Ravenna partisans, posthumously awarded the Silver Medal for Military Valor. Born in 1911 from a family of sharecroppers, Gordini was a member of the federal committee of the Communist Party of Italy in Ravenna. In 1937 he tried in vain to leave Italy to move to Spain and enlist in the International Brigades which fought in support of the republican government against the nationalists. In 1938 the communist farmer was arrested and sentenced to six years in prison. Locked up in Civitavecchia (Province of Rome) Prison until the removal of Benito Mussolini, he devoted himself to the armed struggle after the Italian Armistice. In October 1943 Gordini attempted to kill a Fascist Militia consul. Captured by the Fascists, he was shot in Forlì (Province of Forlì - Cesena) in January 1944.

Intimately connected to the 28th Garibaldi Brigade is the figure of the man who became its commander, Arrigo Boldrini. Born in 1915, in Ravenna like Gordini, Boldrini began working as an agricultural expert. In October 1935 he was called up for military service and sent to the officer cadet school in Fano (Province of Pesaro - Urbino) at the 94th Infantry Regiment *"Messina"*. In May 1936, after completing the course, he was appointed as an aspiring reserve officer and the following month he was assigned to the 11th Infantry Regiment *"Casale"* based in Forlì. In November he was discharged and in 1937 he moved to the reserve roles of the Fascist Militia as a maniple deputy chief. In that same year he began working at the Eridania company in Mezzano (Province of Ravenna). Shortly after, he had his first contacts with communist exponents. He thus began to deal with Marxism and the events of the Spanish civil war but without translating these interests into a concrete political commitment. Left without a job, he enrolled at the Faculty of Economics and Commerce of the University of Bologna in 1939 but failed to graduate.

Although the Voluntary Militia for National Security Command of Ravenna had assigned him to the 121st Legion *"Caio Marzio Coriolano"* in Littoria (today's Latina), Boldrini managed to obtain leave for health reasons. At the end of 1940 he was hired as an employee at the Cerealicoltura of the city in the Lazio region. A few months later he was transferred to the Cerealicoltura section of Padua and subsequently to that of Naples, where he remained until June 1942 when he was called up to arms. In the spring of 1943, he was enlisted with the rank of reserve lieutenant in the 120th Infantry Regiment of *"Emilia"* Division, stationed in Yugoslavia. Having fallen ill, he was granted convalescent leave and on 20 July 1943 he was repatriated to Bari to be hospitalized.

In the Apulian city, on 28 July, just after being discharged and about to return to the barracks, Boldrini came across a group of demonstrators on the run. They were mostly young students and teachers who had marched peacefully to ask for the release of political prisoners. Some units of the Royal Italian Army had shot at the procession, in application of the very harsh provisions issued by General Mario Roatta, confirmed Chief of Staff by the Prime Minister Pietro Badoglio, aimed at repressing any act susceptible to disturb public order. There were 20 deaths and 50 injuries among the demonstrators that day. The young lieutenant from Romagna was deeply shaken by that tragic event and immediately felt the need to return home and evaluate what actions to take for the future. On 8 August, he finally arrived in Ravenna where he came into contact with some important local communist exponents, including Giuseppe D'Alema, father of Massimo who would be President of the Council of Ministers of the Italian Republic from 21 October 1998 to 26 April 2000. After the liberation of Ravenna, Boldrini led the 28th Garibaldi Brigade from December 1944 until its demobilization on 20 May 1945.

He himself revealed how his battle name was born, certainly one of the most legendary in the Italian Resistance, thanks to the idea of a communist barber:

"Michele Pascoli, a history scholar, with whom I have discussed the Napoleonic period and of the emperor's end at Waterloo, imposes on me the nickname of «Bülow» recalling some of my joking and ironic barbs aimed at Napoleon for the defeat of 18 June 1815. For polemical reasons, I contrasted the military genius of the emperor with the ability of the Prussian Friedrich Wilhelm Bülow, who with Gebhard Leberecht Blücher and Wellington was among the architects of the victory of the Anglo-Prussian armies. Michele, with biting irony, also insists that Bülow is pronounced like a dialect word meaning «adventurous, boastful, one who wants to fight». What can I say! I can only accept, without enthusiasm. I really don't like this German nickname. It will then represent a tasty diversion against the various fascists and the Allies, convinced that they are dealing with a defector of Teutonic origin" (*Diario di Bulow*, op. cit.).

On 4 February 1945, in Ravenna, General Richard McCreery, commander of the British 8th Army, pinned the Gold Medal for Military Valor on Arrigo Boldrini's chest. The motivation for the award reads as follows:

"An officer animated by the highest enthusiasm and endowed with exceptional organizational skills, he formed two brigades of patriots in Italian territory occupied by the Germans, which he led for several months in risky and bloody guerrilla actions. In the imminence of the Allied offensive in the area, he sustained at the head of his men and for several consecutive days, hard fighting against strong German garrisons, thus facilitating the task of the Allied armies. Subsequently, with a very daring action, he forced the enemy to abandon an important Adriatic port location that he occupied first. Although violently counterattacked by German armored forces and wounded, he maintained the positions he had conquered, contrasting with inexhaustible tenacity the enemy pressure. He then joined with his men the Anglo-American armies with which he continued the fight for the liberation of the Fatherland.
Ravenna (Porto Corsini), 15 November - 7 December 1944".

After the war, in 1945, Boldrini was elected to the National Council. He was a member of the Constituent Assembly of Italy and the Chamber of Deputies from 1948 to 1976, then a Senator from 1976 to 1994. The communist parliamentarian was also vice-president of the Chamber of Deputies from 1968 to 1976 and twice held the position of vice-president of the Defense Committee of the Chamber of Deputies. He was president of the National Association of Italian Partisans (ANPI) from 1947 to 2006. He died in January 2008.

FORMATION AND OPERATIONS OF THE 28TH GAP (PATRIOTIC ACTION GROUPS) BRIGADE "MARIO GORDINI"

In the last two days of August 1943, a meeting was held at Arrigo Boldrini's house in Ravenna, attended by communist representatives from Alfonsine (Province of Ravenna). The methods of obtaining weapons and the organization of the armed struggle were discussed during the gathering. In the largest city of Romagna the first concrete, though isolated, acts of rebellion against the occupiers took place in the period immediately following the Armistice[1]. Some German soldiers were stopped and disarmed by the partisans who also managed to seize weapons kept in the barracks and warehouses of the city. At the end of September 1943 a provincial military committee of the Communist Party was operational, consisting of Mario Gordini, Gino Gatta (battle name *Zalet*) and Genunzio Guerrini (battle name *Gianò*)[2]. The territory of Ravenna, characterised by the presence of few and not particularly high hills on a vast land dotted with inhabited centers, appeared to the leaders of the resistance unsuitable for conducting large-scale guerrilla warfare such as that practised in the mountains. With the exception of the groups operating in the hills around Forlì, it was almost impossible for numerous partisan units to benefit from safe bases.

Thus the question of *"pianurizzazione"* arose, that is, the opportunity to favour fighting in the plains in any case, where the enemy was located and operating, despite the impossibility of using the most traditional and effective natural defences. Arrigo Boldrini supported this perspective, believing that the rural population would support the Resistance. The rebels' deep knowledge of the area would have allowed them to both attack and defend, taking advantage of the peculiar configuration of the terrain, characterised by rivers, canals and cultivated areas, often delimited by hedges and ditches.

On 29 October 1943, in Ravenna, Mario Gordini attempted an attack on the consul of the Fascist Militia Michele Troiano, commander of the 635th Provincial Command of the National Republican Guard. A few weeks later the first reprisals against the patriots began. That autumn the partisan leaders worked out a more efficient division of the provincial territory through the definition of operational zones (some of which had been planned since July). In order to facilitate the classification

---

1 This is how Arrigo Boldrini remembers the day of the Armistice in Ravenna: *"On the evening of 8 September I go to the café «Grande Italia», in Piazza del Popolo, where before the war many friends used to meet. The club manager, Gigi Laghi, an elderly anti-fascist, kindly advises me to be very careful and since I am armed I give him my service pistol so I can go to Piazza Garibaldi where many citizens are gathering. Bucina (Angelo Siboni), a law student with liberal leaning-beliefs, together with several friends urges me to speak to the crowd. I have a moment of panic and then impulsively speak up, praising the freedom that has been conquered and indicating that the Germans and the fascists must be chased away. A speech? No, a few words but spoken with deep conviction. While the police intervene to charge the demonstrators, Lina Vacchi, a worker at the Callegari factory, helps me escape and takes me by bicycle to Via Oberdan, to the dear friendly family of Antonietta and Ermanno Castaldi"* (Arrigo Boldrini, *Diario di Bulow*, Vangelista Editore, Milano 1985, p. 16).

2 Gino Gatta (*Zalet*) was born in 1909 in Campiano (Province of Ravenna). Listed as a communist, he was forced to take refuge in France in 1937. After returning to Italy he became a member of the federal committee of the Communist Party of Italy in Ravenna, he joined the provincial military committee and became provincial commander of the Partisan Action Squads (SAP). He held the position of political commissioner of the 28th Garibaldi Brigade *"Mario Gordini"*. He was decorated with the Silver Medal of Military Valor in memory in 1983. Genunzio Guerrini (*Gianò*) was born in 1904. A member of the Communist Party of Italy since 1921, he took part in the partisan struggle as political commissioner of the 28th GAP (Patriotic Action Groups) Brigade and of the 28th Garibaldi Brigade *"Mario Gordini"*.

of the partisans, these zones[3] were divided into sectors which corresponded to military and political committees of the Italian Communist Party.

On 22 December 1943 Ilio Barontini[4] (battle name *Dario*), returning from experiences in the field of armed resistance gained in China, Ethiopia, Spain and France, reached Ravenna to meet with Mario Gordini, Gino Gatta and Arrigo Boldrini in order to evaluate the performances of the local partisans. On this occasion the leaders of the Resistance were invited to intensify the fight against the enemy. January 1944 proved particularly tragic: Mario Gordini and Settimio Garavini, leader of the Communist Party, were executed.

At the beginning of the new year, the choice of *"pianurizzazione"* could be said to have been definitively approved. In this context, a sabotage operation began, which resulted in the interruption of telephone lines, the removal of road signs, and the damage to enemy vehicles. A specific attempt was also made to improve the efficiency of the entire Ravenna partisan movement: Boldrini was invited to Lugo (Province of Ravenna) by Tino Baracca, an anti-fascist close to the Giustizia e Libertà movement and related to Francesco Baracca, an ace of the Italian Air Force in the First World War, with the aim of discussing with Giovanni de Lorenzo[5], a monarchist officer of the Royal Italian Army in hiding, regarding the latter's willingness to contribute to the military training of the 8th Garibaldi Brigade, a formation operating in the Romagna Apennines since late autumn 1943. The meeting, however, came to nothing.

In the months of February and March 1944, the GAP (Patriotic Action Groups) of the Ravenna province were able to launch several successful coups. In view of the difficulties associated with implementing a guerrilla warfare in the countryside similar to that typically conducted by the GAP in urban environments, the Ravenna partisan leaders toyed with the idea of forming *"nuclei "volanti"*, namely small units responsible for rapidly striking the enemy by moving from expertly hidden shelters. The first groups of this type were created in April 1944. In the meantime, the 8th Garibaldi Brigade, severely tested by enemy attacks, underwent a forced reorganization and many of its elements were sent to the plains in order to be assigned to new and different tasks.

In late spring preparations began for the creation of a large partisan organization of the Ravenna province, the 28th GAP Brigade[6]. On 7 June 1944 Boldrini met his childhood friend Benigno Zaccagnini (battle name *Tommaso Moro*) in the rectory of the parish church of Piangipane (Province of Ravenna)[7], led by Father Silvio Danesi, who was also present at the meeting, requested by the

---

[3] The operational zones of the Ravenna province were the following: ZONE 1 Ravenna, ZONE 2 Alfonsine, ZONE 3 Lavezzola, ZONE 4/a Conselice, ZONE 4/b Massa Lombarda, ZONE 5 Lugo, ZONE 6 Cervia and Ville Unite, ZONE 7 Bagnacavallo, Fusignano, Russi and Ville Disunite, ZONE 8 Brisighella, Casola Valsenio, Castel Bolognese, Faenza, Riolo Bagni.

[4] In German-occupied France, Ilio Barontini (battle name *Giobbe*) was among the coordinators of the first groups of Francs-tireurs partisans, of which he became Chief of Staff. Returning to Italy after the Armistice, he took the battle name of *Dario* and became a member of the General Command of the Garibaldi Brigades, the partisan formations of the Communist Party. He was responsible for organizing the GAP in the areas occupied by the Nazi-Fascists. From 1944 he was at the head of the CUMER (Unified Military Command Emilia-Romagna).

[5] Giovanni de Lorenzo took part in the Resistance and in 1954 was appointed Brigadier General. He became known for being the head of SIFAR (Armed Forces Information Service) from 1955 to 1962. As General Commander of the Carabinieri, he had the so-called Solo Plan drawn up, to be activated in the event of emergencies regarding public order, which included a list of political figures to be arrested if necessary. From 1966 he was Chief of Staff of the Italian Army but in the following year he was retired due to the deviations resulting from the activity of SIFAR under his direction.

[6] With the establishment of the Brigade it would have taken shape the idea of having a single large partisan organization in the province of Ravenna, directed by a central coordination and provided with a decentralized military structure.

[7] Born in Faenza (province of Ravenna) on 17 April 1912, Benigno Zaccagnini was sent to the Balkans theatre when Italy entered the war. As a reserve Medical Lieutenant of the 121st Infantry Regiment *"Macerata"*, he was awarded the War Cross of Military Valor for distinguishing himself on the Slovenian battlefield on 2 October 1942. Upon returning home he led a Christian Social-inspired resistance movement in Ravenna (which later merged with the Christian Democracy) and from March 1944 he was head of the National Liberation Committee of the province of Ravenna. In 1946 Zaccagnini became

National Liberation Committee of Ravenna. The discussion highlighted the need to achieve greater political-military coordination of the various partisan formations present in the territory. On 25 June 1944 Boldrini and other leaders of the local resistance, including Gaetano Verdelli (battle name *Nando*) and Ennio Cervellati (battle name *Silvio*), initiated the constitution of the Garibaldi Division *"Ravenna"* and proceeded to form the command of the 28th GAP Brigade which was constituted as follows: commander Alberto Bardi (*Falco*), vice-commanders Mario Verlicchi (*Wladimiro*) and Leonida Zannoni (*Leo*), political commissioner Genunzio Guerrini (*Giano*), vice-political commissioner Francesco Verlicchi (*Revel*). Gino Gatta (*Zalet*) and Luigi Bonetti (*Radames*) were appointed commander and political commissioner of the SAP (Partisan Action Squads), respectively[8]. In July 1944 it was decided to name the unit after Mario Gordini. The Brigade's organization was made up of five detachments, each active in well-defined areas, which bore the name of a fallen partisan:

- *"Sauro Babini"*[9] Detachment

Commander: Achille Filippi (*Franco*).
Political Commissioner: Ivo Piolanti (*Annibale*).
The group, made up of 119 partisans, was located between the Lamone and Montone rivers in an area between the towns of Bagnacavallo, Fusignano, Russi and Ville Disunite (province of Ravenna).

- *"Aurelio Tarroni"*[10] Detachment

Commander: Mario Verlicchi (*Wladimiro*).
Political Commissioner: Francesco Ballardini (*Secondo*).
The unit, 130 men strong, operated in an area including the city of Alfonsine which extended between the Lamone and Senio rivers. Mario Verlicchi was, as we have read, also deputy commander of the Brigade and in the autumn of 1944 he had under his command a column made up of fighters from the operational zone of Alfonsine.

- *"Umberto Ricci"*[11] Detachment

---

a member of the Constituent Assembly of Italy (the body that wrote the Italian Constitution). From 1948 to 1983 he was a member of the Italian Chamber of Deputies and from 1983 to 1989 he held the office of Senator. During his political career, Zaccagnini was Minister of Labour and Social Security from 15 February 1959 to 25 March 1960 and Minister of Public Works from 26 March 1960 to 21 February 1962. From 1975 to 1980 he was national secretary of the Christian Democracy.

8 The command of the whole *"Ravenna"* Division would have been entrusted to Boldrini. It is important to remember that the CUMER and other political and military entities of the Emilia-Romagna Resistance never officially recognized the existence of a Division that should have included lower level units such as the SAP or the 28th GAP Brigade. Shortly after, a Battalion was formed, also called *"Ravenna"*, in the area of Brisighella and Riolo Bagni (province of Ravenna), to meet the needs related to mountain guerrilla warfare. After having conducted several actions in the plains, this unit was attached to the 8th Garibaldi Brigade.

9 Sauro Babini (battle name *Cetriolo*), was born in 1925 in Roncalceci (province of Ravenna). Having joined the 8th Garibaldi Brigade (2nd Company), he fell in combat on 16 March 1944. He was awarded the Silver Medal of Military Valor in memory.

10 Worker of communist belief and partisan, Aurelio Tarroni was born in Alfonsine in 1907. Captured near Fusignano, he was shot in Ravenna on 23 April 1944. After the war he was decorated with the Silver Medal of Military Valor in memory.

11 The Detachment was named after Umberto Ricci (*Napoleone*) only after 25 August 1944. On that date, the GAP member from Massa Lombarda (Province of Ravenna) was executed by the militia of the Italian Social Republic together with Natalina (Lina) Vacchi (*La Bionda*), a communist worker and partisan courier who played a decisive role in preventing Boldrini's arrest on 8 September 1943. Umberto Ricci was decorated with the Silver Medal, Natalina Vacchi with the Bronze Medal.

Commander: Hidalgo Tampieri (*Lampo*).
Political Commissioner: Silvio Pasi (*Erlic*).
Active in an area delimited by the Senio and Santerno rivers which included the cities of Conselice, Lavezzola, Massa Lombarda (province of Ravenna) and partly the town of Lugo, the formation had a strength of 106 men.

- ❖ *"Celso Strocchi"*[12] Detachment

Commander: Sesto Liverani (*Palì*).
Political Commissioner: Mario Badiali (*Mario*).

This detachment operated in an area enclosed between the Santerno and Lamone rivers, which included the towns of Brisighella, Casola Valsenio, Castel Bolognese, Cotignola, Faenza, Lugo, Riolo Bagni (province of Ravenna) and was made up of 104 partisans.

- ❖ *"Settimio Garavini"*[13] Detachment

Commander: Primo Bandini (*Noco*).
Political Commissioner: Angelo Giovannetti (*Il Moro*).

The unit, with 137 men, operated in the vast area of the province of Ravenna called Ville Unite, located south of the Fiumi Uniti, watercourse generated by the confluence of Ronco and Montone rivers, and in the vicinity of Cervia (province of Ravenna). It grouped together formations that had been operating south of Ravenna since September 1943. After Bandini's death, which occurred at the end of October 1944, the *"Garavini"* Detachment was placed at the orders of Ateo Minghelli (*Règan*)[14]. Each detachment was officially divided in squads of 16 men, nuclei of 8 men and groups of 4 men. On 1 August 1944, in order to be able to count on a partisan force in the plains closer to the cities, capable of providing possible support to other patriot units, a sixth detachment was formed which took the name of Terzo Lori[15], fallen partisan of the 8th Garibaldi Brigade. The *"Terzo Lori"* Detachment had to settle in the overwhelmed case of Lamone River, a humid and somewhat unhealthy environment, among the reeds and the banks of the watercourse. The area of deployment of the unit extended between the Strada Romea (a road incomplete and impassable in some sections) and the road that connected the main town of Romagna with Cà di Bosco and Sant'Alberto (province of Ravenna). The command of the Detachment was composed as follows: commander Ulisse Ballotta (*Alfio*), from Alfonsine, deputy commander Sebastiano Casali (*Tito*), political commissioner Lino Bartolotti (*Roberto*), deputy political commissioner Andrea Montanari (*Jonio*).

---

12 Celso Strocchi, member of the communist provincial military committee, partisan expert in armaments, took part in the first armed actions in Ravenna. On the day of the attack on the Fascist Militia Consul Michele Troiano, Strocchi was together with Mario Gordini. Imprisoned, he was eliminated with a pistol shot.

13 Settimio Garavini was born in 1914 in Castiglione di Ravenna. By profession bricklayer, he was a leader of the communist partisan movement in Ville Unite. Captured together with Mario Gordini, he was shot by the Fascists on 14 January 1944.

14 Immediately after Bandini's death the *"Garavini"* Detachment was temporarily commanded by Brunetto Paganelli (*Giorgio*).

15 Born on 4 July 1913 in Alfonsine, Terzo Lori served as political commissioner of a company of the 8th Garibaldi Brigade *"Romagnola"*, later renamed *"Romagna"*. He fell in combat at Biserno di Santa Sofia (Province of Forlì-Cesena) on 11 April 1944. His sacrifice was rewarded with a Gold Medal. It's safe to say that the *"Terzo Lori"* Detachment was the only amphibious unit of the Italian Resistance. The well-known journalist from Ravenna Sergio Zavoli edited a documentary for *Rai* (the national public broadcasting company of Italy) entitled *"L'armata delle valli"*, broadcast in 1966, which collects the precious testimonies of important exponents of the *"Lori"* Detachment and other formations attributable to the *"Gordini"* Brigade.

The first successful actions were conducted mainly at night. The German back lines were heavily hit. On 21 September 1944, Pietro Gaudenzi (*Bruno*), replaced *Alfio*, afflicted by health problems, in command of the *"Lori"* Detachment. Andrea Montanari became political commissioner. During the night of 29 September, various bridges, including the one on the Lamone River along the road between Sant'Alberto and Ravenna, were hit by the partisans. The rising waters in the area where the *"Terzo Lori"* Detachment was quartered made it essential to transfer several squads to nearby and, in a certain sense, more hospitable areas. A group chose a small island, called *"degli Spinaroni"*[16], as their operational base, a place that was practically inaccessible in the absence of suitable means to cross numerous channels. The men had to adapt to living in holes concealed by camouflage tarps and the headquarters were established in a fishing hut. Incredibly, the Germans never managed to correctly locate the partisan camp. Radio communications with the Allies took place twice a day, at 10:00 and 16:00. The islet also housed a depot for supplies and a medical post[17]. Professor Alfredo Badiali joined the partisans and, assisted by his son Carlo, a medical student, became the responsible medical specialist of the formation. Many of the men who flocked to the *"Lori"* Detachment lacked military knowledge. Such a gap was tackled with an innovative spirit: it was necessary to acquire the necessary experience in the field.

The Detachment was later joined by some foreigners, Soviet deserters from the German Army and a French soldier, with whom the Italians immediately established an excellent understanding. Pietro Gaudenzi narrates that the weapons were initially largely stolen from the enemy and only later obtained thanks to the Allies[18].

By early October 1944, the German deployment north of Ravenna was significantly strengthened. A complex and articulated defensive system blocked access to the city to the south along the course of the Fiumi Uniti, to the east near the Adriatic coast and to the north along the course of the Lamone River. Artillery positions, interruptions of fords, demolitions of bridges, flooding of the land, minefields and fortifications constituted an almost insurmountable barrier. The *"Gordini"* Brigade command insisted with the Allies to receive further supplies.

On 20 October the matter of the liberation of Ravenna was addressed for the first time, an objective that could be achieved only thanks to the approval of a plan agreed with the British that would have contemplated the annihilation of the German garrisons present north of the town. The Brigade detachments had to prepare for the imminent action. The *"Lori"* had at that time 135 men distributed across 5 companies, each divided into 3 squads. Every day, one of the companies, in turn, was given a specific task that could range from reconnaissance to ambush missions. During the night hours the patrols of the *"Lori"* Detachment were mainly employed in missions on the Via Reale (Highway 16) to hit the German motorised columns on the move. The *"Lori"* Detachment's privileged objective was Porto Corsini (Ravenna), a nearby enemy stronghold with particularly well-fortified defenses. On 31 October 1944 the British command requested that a company of partisans from the *"Garavini"* Detachment join the *No 1 Demolition Squadron* better known as *Popski's Private Army*,

---

16 In the local dialect, this name identifies the sea buckthorn, a plant that once covered the entire surface of the islet, located in the Piallassa della Baiona, a brackish lagoon north of Ravenna.

17 The logistical problem was solved thanks to the precious contribution of the civilian population. Every day, defying the adverse environmental conditions, various boats led by civilians landed at Spinaroni Island with their precious cargoes.

18 Commander Gaudenzi recalled that at Porto Corsini (Ravenna) 2 machine guns were captured. On 12 November 1944 the partisans also seized a gun (equipped with 72 rounds). It was most likely an Italian 47/32 anti-tank gun that was widely used in the continuation of the operations. The piece, camouflaged in white according to a veteran, apparently got lost in the area around Mandriole (Ravenna), south of the Comacchio Valleys. A radio station was present on Spinaroni Island from October 1944. In fact, a mission code-named *"Bionda"* operated in support of the partisans, consisting of the radiotelegrapher Giuseppe Montanino, the second lieutenant Angelo Garrone and the Marine Antonio Maletto. The three Italian soldiers belonged to the *"San Marco"* Regiment (Paratrooper Swimmers). Another radio station serving the partisans was that of the *"Elvira"* Group, active since 19 July 1944.

led by Wladimir Peniakoff (*Popski*)[19]. If Ravenna had been subjected to intense bombing, the consequences on the population and the artistic heritage would have been devastating. The liberation of the city seemed achievable and so Arrigo Boldrini believed that the time had come to explain his point of view to the Allied command. On the night of 18 November 1944, *Bülow* and some of his comrades set sail from the coast of Porto Corsini and at 7:00 the next day they landed in Milano Marittima (province of Ravenna). Having reached Viserba (Rimini), Boldrini took part in several meetings with the head of the intelligence service of the headquarters of the Canadian I Corps led by General Charles Foulkes and with other officers of the British 8th Army headquarters. The partisan commander was then able to explain to his interlocutors the specifics of the operational plan he had drawn up:

1) The *"Gordini"* sub-units were supposed to launch lightning-fast and forceful attacks, moving from different directions to give the enemy the impression of being attacked from several sides, taking advantage of the peculiarities of the terrain given by the presence of valleys, the lack of practicable communication routes, and the banks of watercourses.

2) The Allies were to conduct the main offensive against the Germans and maintain constant contact with the partisan commands.

---

19 Wladimir Peniakoff was born in Belgium to parents of Russian origin in 1897. A former artilleryman in the French Army during the Great War, at the outbreak of the Second World War he volunteered in the British army with the rank of second lieutenant. Appointed commander of a company in the *Libyan Arab Force* (a unit structured into 5 battalions of volunteers, mainly Libyans who had taken refuge in Egypt), he fought in the vicinity of Tobruk. In May 1942 he was placed in charge of the *Libyan Arab Force Commando*, a nimble formation consisting of 22 Senussi, 1 Arab officer and 1 British sergeant, active in the mountainous area of Jebel Akhdar, located between Benghazi and Derna. It was Colonel Shan Hackett, supervisor of the British special forces in the Middle East, who tasked Peniakoff with creating a small motorized unit capable of wreaking havoc in the rear areas of the Axis, which would be called *No. 1 Demolition Squadron*. This name did not please Peniakoff, who in the meantime had taken the nickname of *Popski*, given to him by the New Zealanders of the *Long Range Desert Group* (a special unit of His Majesty's Army created in Egypt in 1940, under the direct command of General Archibald Wavell, charged with carrying out long-range reconnaissance, made up of men from all over the British Empire and equipped with vehicles appropriately modified for the tasks to be carried out, especially jeeps and trucks) with whom he had cooperated. Hackett then proposed to baptize the tiny group as *Popski's Private Army*. In October 1942, it consisted of only 17 men, equipped with 4 Jeeps armed with twin 7.7 mm Vickers machine guns and 2 3-ton trucks used to transport food rations, explosives and fuel. In North Africa, Peniakoff's "corsairs" ambushed enemy convoys, destroyed aircraft on the ground at airfields and struck weapons and fuel depots. On 9 September 1943 *Popski's Private Army* landed at Taranto together with elements of the British 1st Airborne Division. With 5 Jeeps rearmed with American Cal. 30 and Cal. 50 machine guns, *Popski* also operated behind German lines in Italy. On one occasion, his men routed a group of German engineers intent on mining a ford on the Fortore River. The passage was taken and held to allow the transit of tanks of the British 4th Armoured Brigade to the north. In the autumn of 1943, Major Peniakoff, supported by 2 captains and 3 lieutenants, had 74 men at his orders. The equipment was also enriched, allowing the establishment of headquarters, 1 mechanical workshop, 1 signal section, 1 administrative section and 3 patrols of 6 Jeeps. Each patrol included 1 officer, 1 sergeant, 2 corporals, 1 mechanic, 1 radio operator and 6 drivers/machine gunners. *Popski* met the Italian partisans for the first time in the Marche region, more precisely in Bolognola, a small town near Sarnano (Province of Macerata). The combined actions with the local patriots were mainly aimed at hitting the German columns moving along the course of Chienti River. By mid-September 1944 the Allies had broken through the Gothic Line but the enemy's opposition had not weakened and was relying on the natural obstacles provided by the dense network of waterways that crossed the territory. *Popski* then thought of training his men to use the *DUKWs*, the famous amphibious trucks of American production. On 1 November, after crossing the Savio River, Peniakoff's men ran into a group of partisans from the 28th GAP Brigade *"Mario Gordini"*, under the command of Ateo Minghelli (*Règan*). Thus a strong partnership was born between the GAP members and *Popski*'s specialists. Patriots were attached to each patrol of *No 1 Demolition Squadron*. The collaboration between the British and the Italians worked very well. In addition to the 2 on-board machine guns that armed the Jeeps, each patrol was equipped with 2 Bren machine guns, 1 bazooka and 1 2-inch mortar. On 4 December 1944, *Popski's Private Army* and part of the *"Garavini"* Detachment were among the first formations to enter Ravenna. At that time, during a tough clash with the Germans, Wladimir Peniakoff lost his left hand and was temporarily replaced in command of the unit by the French captain Jean Caneri. From 21 to 28 April 1945, the British in Jeeps and the *Garibaldini* from Romagna fought with great determination in the waters of the Comacchio Lagoon (north of Ravenna) against the Germans. Having crossed the Po and Adige rivers, the *Popski's Private Army* was able to capture hundreds of prisoners. In Chioggia (province of Venice) *Popski* rejoined his soldiers. After parading on their Jeeps in Piazza San Marco in Venice, the group under the command of the indomitable major of the British Army moved towards Austria where, at the end of the conflict, was disbanded.

British Intelligence Major Archibald Coulquhoun and Captain John Francis Rendall from London were very interested in Boldrini's proposal. According to Rendall, the protection of Ravenna's artistic heritage should not be subordinated to the requirements of the war. From this intention was born the code name *"Teodora"*[20], assigned to the operation and inspired by the name of the Byzantine empress portrayed on the mosaics of the Basilica of San Vitale, proposed by the English captain himself. The enemy had prepared the defense of Ravenna, now almost deserted. The Germans and fascists exploited the high banks of the Montone and Ronco rivers to the south and at the confluence of the two waterways, that of the Fiumi Uniti. To the north, the Lamone River helped the defenders because its waters were above the safety level and fortifications had been erected along the coast to counter possible landings. One of the most singular episodes that occurred in the period immediately preceding the beginning of Operation *"Teodora"* undoubtedly concerns the liberation of the Basilica of Sant'Apollinare in Classe[21], located a few kilometers south of the Romagna capital.

Some partisans of the *"Garavini"* Detachment including Ateo Minghelli (*Régan*) having learned that the Allies intended to hit the church bell tower, used as an observation post by the Germans, wanted to prevent its destruction. Wladimir Peniakoff immediately sided with the patriots with whom he had been collaborating for a long time, and did everything possible to postpone the bombing. During the night between 18 and 19 November 1944, a patrol of 35 men, 25 from *Popski's Private Army* and 10 from the *"Garavini"* Detachment, moved towards the village of Classe (Ravenna). At dawn, the group burst into the town and the machine guns that armed Peniakoff's Jeeps opened fire on any possible target, targeting windows, doors and roofs of the buildings with the intent of hitting any enemy soldier who had found shelter in them. The partisans of the *"Garavini"* Detachment managed to enter the Basilica which, however, had been abandoned by the enemy. Some Germans surrendered, others fled. Sant'Apollinare was saved.

▲ Partisans of the *"Terzo Lori"* Detachment. Spinaroni's Island, summer 1944.

---

20 Theodora (about 500 – Constantinople, 28 June 548), wife of Emperor Justinian I, was perhaps the most famous of the Byzantine empresses. After her husband's death in 525, she reigned alone for about twenty years.

21 The early Paleochristian basilica was erected in the VI century after Christ by order of Bishop Ursicino and was dedicated to the Patron Saint of Ravenna. Its destruction was avoided by the victorious and daring action conducted jointly by *Popski*'s men and the patriots of *"Garavini"* Detachment (*"Così noi e Popsky liberammo Sant'Apollinare"*, edited by Ivano Artioli, https://www.anpi.it/patria-indipendente/media/uploads/patria/2005/9/31-32_ARTIOLI.pdf). Classe is the name of the locality south of Ravenna where the place of worship stands.

▲ Posed photograph of partisans of the *"Terzo Lori"* Detachment. Spinaroni's Island, September 1944.

▼ Men of the 28th GAP Brigade immortalized during a moment of rest after a patrol. Pineta di Classe (Province of Ravenna), autumn 1944.

▲ Partisan of the 28th GAP Brigade. The woman is armed with a Steyr – Pieper pistol, (model 1909 probably), of Austrian production. This photograph was taken south of Ravenna on 18 November 1944.

▲ Partisan of the 28th GAP Brigade tasked with observing enemy movements from a lookout post.

▲ Ateo Minghelli (also known as *Règan*, a battle name that literally translated from the dialect of Romagna means Hurricane) talks to a female partisan, also belonging to the 28th GAP Brigade *"Gordini"*. They both wear the typical British *battledress* jacket. Pineta di Classe (Province of Ravenna), autumn 1944.

▲ The same female partisan in the previous image poses for the photographer holding a Beretta model 1938 submachine gun.

▼ A partisan of the *"Garavini"* Detachment photographed in Pineta di Classe (Province of Ravenna).

THE LIBERATION OF RAVENNA & THE "BATTLE OF THE VALLEYS"

On 21 November 1944 Boldrini visited the *"Garavini"* Detachment, which was mainly made up of young partisans, including some women who performed auxiliary functions[22].
On the same day *Bulow* also visited *Popski*'s headquarters, housed inside an old building on the Strada Romea. The British officer did not hide his concerns about the slowdown of operations, held back by the poor state of the communication routes, the flooded land and the minefields but he expressed his firm intention to liberate Ravenna with the collaboration of the Italian patriots.
At the end of November the *"Gordini"* Brigade was attached to the Canadian I Corps. The partisan command of Alfonsine had in the meantime arranged for the placement of the GAP and SAP of the Operational Zone 2 at the orders of Mario Verlicchi. The grouping, which became known as the *"Wladimiro"* Column from the battle name of its commander[23], also included the *"Tarroni"* Detachment and boasted a total strength of about 400 men.
The Canadian Captain Healy, sent to the 28th GAP Brigade, arranged the methods of connection with his command. Late in the evening a message from the Allies arrived, specifying the role of the partisans on the eve of the offensive, that of occupation troops in the sector that went from Mezzano (Ravenna) to the coast, up to the Comacchio Valleys (located between the provinces of Ravenna and Ferrara). During the night between 2 and 3 December 1944, the signal *"Zero Hour"* reached the GAP members via radio. Thus began a clash known as the *"Battle of the Valleys"*, which took place north of Ravenna until 6 December 1944.
The patriots had to prepare to attack from Sant'Alberto to the coast at the moment in which the 8th Army would have started Operation *"Chuckle"* which envisaged the use of the Canadian I Corps on the extreme right of the front, of the British V Corps on the Faenza - Bologna route in the centre, of the Polish II Corps on the left flank in the area of the Romagna hills. Tasks strictly related to the liberation of Ravenna had been assigned to the *Porterforce*[24], to the *Popski's Private Army* and to the *"Garavini"* Detachment.
On 4 December 1944, at dawn, almost 1,000 partisans launched their attack. They were the men of the *"Terzo Lori"* Detachment, of the *"Sauro Babini"* Detachment and of the other sub-units included in the *"Wladimiro"* Column, of two SAP group from Alfonsine and Ravenna, of some GAP formations that arrived from Conselice and Massa Lombarda. The *"Lori"* Detachment was charged with taking over the localities of Porto Corsini, Casal Borsetti and Mandriole (Ravenna), the *"Wladimiro"* Column was instead supposed to take Sant'Alberto and hinder the enemy's retreat towards Ferrara.

---

22 The whole partisan Detachment was operationally assigned to the *No 1 Demolition Squadron*. The high regard expressed by Wladimir Peniakoff for the *"Garavini"* Detachment is reflected in the following written statement:
"The Settimio Garavini partisan group has operated with us during the last six weeks, taking part in all the actions to which it was called. We can state, in all truth, that without the excellent cooperation that we have received at all times from the commanders and patriots and the very high sense of courage and devotion to duty demonstrated tirelessly at every opportunity, our work in this sector would have been very difficult if not impossible.
The commanding officer wishes to express his gratitude to Ateo and the entire Settimio Garavini group for everything they have done during this period".

Major Commanding
No. 1 Demolition Squadron
PPA Special Forces
(Major Popski)

23 The *"Wladimiro"* Column also included 8 partisans from Ferrara and 3 Czechoslovakian soldiers who abandoned the German battalion in which they had been enlisted (Arrigo Boldrini, *Diario di Bulow*, op. cit., p. 162).

24 The *Porterforce* was a battle group of the British 8th Army consisting of armoured, infantry, artillery and engineer units.

The Germans, ready to face an offensive from the south, were unable to counter attacks from other directions and retreated towards the towns of Longastrino[25], Alfonsine and beyond the Comacchio Valleys. The plan initially seemed to be successful and Ravenna was liberated. The partisans entered the city cautiously, taking care not to be hit by the fire of delaying enemy troops. Together with them were elements of the Canadian I Corps.

Meanwhile, the *"Battle of the Valleys"* went on. On 5 December the situation was assessed: losses were limited but ammunition began to run low. That day Italo Cristofori (*Nadir*), Chief of Staff of the *"Babini"* Detachment, fell in the battle[26], wound to death as he was preparing to return to his men after a reconnaissance action. Despite the difficulties, on 6 December the *"Wladimiro"* Column managed to occupy Sant'Alberto. However, no signal arrived from the Allies and the Germans prepared to counterattack from the early hours of the afternoon[27]. The clashes continued until late at night. Repeated requests for air intervention formulated by the partisans were rejected by the British due to the persistence of a thick fog on the battlefield. Sant'Alberto and Mandriole were thus abandoned to the enemy.

▲ Jeeps of Allied units stop waiting to cross the Fiumi Uniti. The remains of the Ponte Nuovo, destroyed by the Germans, emerge from the waters. Ravenna, 4 December 1944.

---

25 The municipality of Longastrino is divided between the municipalities of Alfonsine and Argenta, and therefore between the provinces of Ravenna and Ferrara.

26 Italo Cristofori was born in Bagnacavallo (province of Ravenna) in 1921. Active in the ranks of the Resistance after the Armistice, he was awarded the Silver Medal of Military Valor posthumously.

27 According to Boldrini, who was slightly wounded during the enemy counterattack, enemy forces consisted of sub-units of the 42nd German Jäger Division and elements of the LXXVI Panzer Korps (Arrigo Boldrini, *Diario di Bulow*, op. cit., p. 168).

▲ A Jeep is ferried across the Fiumi Uniti. Ravenna was liberated by troops of the I Canadian Corps.

▼ Allied Jeeps enter Ravenna.

▲ Partisans photographed in Piazza del Popolo in Ravenna immediately after the liberation of the city.

▼ Two partisans guard a group of German prisoners. Ravenna, 5 December 1944.

▲ Canadian Captain Dennis Healy, liaison officer at the *"Terzo Lori"* Detachment, illustrates to the partisans the functioning of a Panzerfaust, the well-known portable anti-tank weapon of the German Army. In the background, the outline of an immobilized German Panther medium tank can be seen.

▼ Wladimir Peniakoff in the driver's seat of a Jeep.

▲ Members of *Popski's Private Army* (PPA) pose in front of some Jeeps of the unit.

▼ A PPA Jeep armed with two machine guns (Cal. .30 and Cal. .50) crosses a stream.

▲ *Popski's Private Army* men and vehicles. The photograph features 3-ton Canadian Military Pattern (CMP) trucks and Dodge D15s, as well as a Jeep armed with machine guns.

▼ A Jeep from the unit commanded by Wladimir Peniakoff passes through Piazza San Marco in Venice.

▲ The only Jeep of *Popski's Private Army* armed with a Wasp Mk II flamethrower. Wladimir Peniakoff, standing right, carefully observes the vehicle. The modification, implemented and tested during the Italian campaign, did not give satisfactory results.

▼ A Jeep of *Popski's Private Army* bearing the stylized symbol of the unit, a 16th century Italian astrolabe, on the front. The badge, which also adorned the headgear of the soldiers of the unit, was designed by the highly decorated Paolo Caccia Dominioni, an officer of the Royal Italian Army and partisan as well as a friend of Wladimir Peniakoff.

▲ In the center of the photograph, Ilario Tabarri (*Pietro Mauri*), commander of the 8th Garibaldi Brigade. Note on the jacket the rank insignia, an inverted triangle in cloth of an unspecified color with three stars, of a darker shade (perhaps red) and of identical size. A similar badge also identified the brigade political commissioner.

▼ Deployment of the 8th Garibaldi Brigade in Forlì on 30 November 1944. Captured machine guns are positioned in front of the partisans.

▲ Gino Larice (*Tigrotto*), young standard-bearer of the 8th Garibaldi Brigade *"Romagna"*.

▲ German machine guns captured by partisans of the 8th Garibaldi Brigade.

▼ A parade of the 8th Garibaldi Brigade was held in Forlì on 30 November 1944. The photograph shows, from left to right, Commander Ilario Tabarri, Gino Larice, the very young standard-bearer of the formation, who wears a British Mk II helmet and a German belt, and political commissioner Pietro Reali (*Bernardo*). All three are wearing British uniforms. The man partially visible on the right may be a liaison officer of Her Majesty as he carries on his sleeve the emblem of the 1st British Armoured Division, a white rhinoceros on a black background.

▲ Two partisans of the 8th Garibaldi Brigade photographed in Forlì on 30 November 1944. The rank insignia adopted by the partisans could vary significantly from one formation to another and it is not easy to trace the actual hierarchical position of these men, considering the different sizes of the stars and the shape of the triangles. The badge applied to the cap of the patriot on the left, a tricolor star probably, is interesting.

▼ Another photograph depicting patriots of the 8th Garibaldi Brigade. Note the heterogeneity of the clothing.

▲ *"Acorn Inn"*, a self-propelled 75mm gun M3 half-track of the 27th Lancers, in action north-west of Mezzano, (Province of Ravenna), on 18 February 1945.

▼ Sexton 25 pdr self propelled gun of 1st Regiment Royal Horse Artillery, operating as part of *"Porterforce"*, on the Adriatic coast near Ravenna on 1 December 1944.

▲ Soldiers of the British 27th Lancers reconnaissance regiment photographed in Ravenna on 5 December 1944.

▼ Sherman V medium tanks of the 5th Canadian Armoured Brigade pass through the streets of Ravenna. January 1945.

THE 28ᵀᴴ GARIBALDI BRIGADE "MARIO GORDINI"

Immediately after the liberation of Ravenna, the patriots expressed their will to continue the fight against the Nazi-Fascists. The British, on the contrary, insisted on employing the rebels mainly in sabotage and covert actions, underestimating the importance that the Italian Resistance had assumed by the end of 1944.

However, some Allied officers were of a different opinion. The Canadian Major Healy seconded to the *"Lori"* Detachment, Wladimir Peniakoff, Major Coulquhoun and General Charles Foulkes held in high regard the reasons of the partisans, fighters who had fought with great courage alongside the Allied troops. Also Corps General Angelo Cerica, former commander of the Carabinieri and Colonel of Cavalry Riccardo Esclapon di Villanova, both of the Royal Italian Army, in liaison with the Anglo-American forces, supported the patriots' claims. After several meetings and intense negotiations, Ravenna resistance fighters and representatives of the 8ᵗʰ Army reached an agreement that provided for the presence of a British liaison officer at the *"Gordini"* Brigade, a formation to which a section of the frontline would be assigned. The men of the detachments that were sent to Ravenna had to hand over their weapons, a measure that did not fail to provoke heated discussions[28].

In Ravenna, on 10 December 1944, Benigno Zaccagnini, president of the local National Liberation Committee, and Arrigo Boldrini held a speech in front of a crowd to urge the recruitment of volunteers in the *"Gordini"* Brigade. The demonstration achieved the desired results and many young people showed up to enlist, but it also led to some misunderstanding with the Allies who complained that they had not been informed of the initiative. From mid-December the new recruits were concentrated in Ravenna[29]. The sub-units that would make up the new structure of the partisan Brigade would be subject to a review process that would make them similar to regular units. Companies of 33-36 men were thus formed, divided into three teams. The commander and the political commissioner would be elected by the members of the company. Command of the *"Gordini"* Brigade was assumed by Arrigo Boldrini. Gino Gatta assumed the role of political commissioner, Ateo Minghelli (*Règan*) and Mario Verlicchi (*Wladimiro*) were appointed deputy commanders, Pellegrino Montanari (*Rino*) became Chief of Staff, Alfredo and Carlo Badiali were placed in charge of the personnel assigned to the Medical services. The renewed organization of the partisan unit, which transformed from GAP Brigade into Garibaldi Brigade, was centered on 15 companies in addition to the headquarters Company and various services.

The arrival of the Lieutenant General of the Realm Umberto II of Savoy in Ravenna on 19 December 1944 further consolidated the status of the *"Gordini"* Brigade with the Anglo-Americans. On the same day the Germans attacked on the Alfonsine-Ravenna road. Partisans and Allies repelled the offensive. The 1ˢᵗ Canadian Infantry Division had meanwhile been launched to conquer Bagnacavallo. The city, liberated on 21 December, was preserved from a massive Allied bombing thanks to two local patriots, Mario Giacomoni and Bruno Cristofori[30]. Giacomoni (battle name *Portos*) convinced

---

[28] The *"Garavini"* Detachment followed the Allied units moving north, replacing patriot formations that had been severely tested by the "Battle of the Valleys" and had been transferred to Ravenna for a period of rest.

[29] The intention of the *"Gordini"* Brigade headquarters was to unite in a single company volunteers coming from the same areas for obvious reasons of understanding.

[30] Mario Giacomoni was born in Prati di Bagnacavallo (Province of Ravenna) on 17 June 1924. Until the spring of 1944 he was a member of the 8ᵗʰ Garibaldi Brigade, active in the Forlì Apennines. Upon returning to his hometown, he joined the local partisans and then he enlisted in the *"Gordini"* Brigade in the autumn of 1944. He held the position of political commissioner, first in the *"Babini"* Detachment and then in the 3ʳᵈ Company of the 28ᵗʰ Garibaldi Brigade and was awarded the Silver Medal of Military Valor. After the war he was a city councilor, assessor and mayor of Bagnacavallo. Bruno Cristofori

the Canadians to postpone the artillery barrage that would have certainly destroyed the town by at least a couple of days. He himself assured the Allies that he would cross the lines during the night to test the real strength of the German defenses. After swimming across the Lamone River, Giacomoni and Cristofori cautiously ventured into the streets of Bagnacavallo in the darkness, finding temporary refuge in the parish priest's house.

Having obtained the much desired information, they quickly returned to the rear and managed to convince the Canadian command of the uselessness of a mass sustained artillery fire. At the end of the year the morale of the partisans suffered a serious blow: the *"Celso Strocchi"* Detachment was disbanded by the Allies without warning. With the new year the recruitment of volunteers continued. Many of them had already been part of the SAP or the GAP. Others, too young, had never been trained. There were thousands of applications for enlistment, an unexpected quantity, a consequence of the great enthusiasm that pervaded many young people from the province of Ravenna. On 9 January 1945 the *"Gordini"* Brigade was assigned to the Canadian I Corps. The new clothing consisting of British uniforms finally arrived and the armament was completed. The partisans were mainly supplied with Lee Enfield rifles, Thompson submachine guns, Bren machine guns, PIAT (Projector Infantry Anti-Tank) anti-tank grenade launchers.

▲ Soldiers of the *"Royal Canadian Dragoons"* armored regiment aboard a Dingo light armored car talk with partisans Bruno and Luisa Cristofori. Bagnacavallo (Province of Ravenna), 3 January 1945.

(known as *Giuseppone*), brother of Italo, Chief of Staff of the *"Babini"* Detachment, was born in Bagnacavallo in 1926.

▲ Another picture of the meeting between the partisans of Bagnacavallo and the Canadian soldiers. Luisa Cristofori holds a Thompson M1929 submachine gun.

▼ Men of the *"Settimio Garavini"* Detachment cross the Bevano River.

▲ A picture of Canadian General Charles Foulkes.

▲ Partisans of the 28th Garibaldi Brigade loading ammunition into a German-made IF-8 trailer. Bank of the Reno River, January 1945.

▼ Patriots of the *"Mario Gordini"* Brigade about to conduct a reconnaissance mission.

▲ Partisans of the *"Gordini"* Brigade familiarize themselves with the new weapons obtained from the Allies.

▼ Peasants in their ox-drawn cart pass a knocked-out German Panther tank. Sant'Alberto (Ravenna), February 1945.

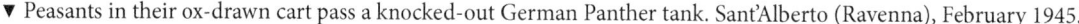

THE "MARIO GORDINI" BRIGADE ENTERS THE FRONT LINE

On 12 January 1945 the Brigade received order to move quickly to the first line to guard and defend the section of front (approximately 3.5 kilometres long) that ran along the course of the Reno River from Sant'Alberto to Casa Strelga. The first companies (4th, 5th, 8th, 9th and 10th Company) that reached their destination were stationed in farmhouses and in improvised defensive positions set up close of the river. Communications between the sub-units were made using field telephones, distress signals made with Very pistols and couriers. In order to avoid possible interceptions by the Germans, telephone communications took place in local dialect. On 14 January at 6:00 the *"Cremona"* Combat Group entered the line[31]. The Italian co-belligerent unit attached to the British 8th Army assumed tactical responsibility for the section of the front line from Mezzano to the Adriatic Sea. About 5 of the more than 20 km that constituted this front (along the right bank of the Reno River and the southern shore of the Comacchio lagoon) were assigned to the *"Gordini"* Brigade which thus found itself deployed between two sub-units of the Italian Combat Group, specifically the III Battalion of the 22nd Infantry Regiment on the right and the I Battalion of the same regiment on the left.

On 17 January 1945 Arrigo Boldrini and other important members of the 28th Garibaldi Brigade left for Rome. In the capital city of Italy, the Ravenna delegation met Francesco Leone, at the time Deputy Head of Press and Propaganda Activities of the Communist Party in Rome, Alessandro Vaia, former commander of a partisan division in the Marche region and representative of the Garibaldi Brigades within the National Partisan Association and Giancarlo Pajetta, nicknamed *Nullo*, communist leader and important personality of the National Liberation Committee of Northern Italy, charged with dealing with the Italian government and the Allies. Together with Pajetta, *Bülow* was then received by the Minister of War, the liberal Alessandro Casati[32].

The executive had decided to recognize the Corpo Volontari della Libertà (the military structure of the Resistance) as an integral part of the Italian co-belligerent Army. It was at that moment that Arrigo Boldrini learned that the Allies had proposed to decorate him with the Gold Medal of Military Valor. The award ceremony for the prestigious recognition was held in Ravenna on 4 February 1945.

As the first month of the new year drew to a close, clashes continued between opposing patrols at the front. At 13:00 on 22 January, the 1st Company of the *"Gordini"* Brigade opened fire on a small

---

[31] The *"Cremona"* Combat Group was constituted as described below:
- Headquarters
- 21st Infantry Regiment (3 battalions, 1 anti-tank company, 1 mortar company)
- 22nd Infantry Regiment (3 battalions, 1 anti-tank company, 1 mortar company)
- 7th Artillery Regiment (4 25-pounders groups, 1 anti-tank group, 1 anti-aircraft group)
- 144th Mixed Engineer Battalion (2 engineer companies and 1 signal company)
- 54th Medical Section
- 84th Field Hospital
- 333rd Field Hospital
- 44th Transport and Supply Unit
- Mechanical Workshops
- Mobile Depot for Artillery and Engineer Materials
- 94th Carabinieri Section
- 739th Carabinieri Section
- 51st British Liaison Unit.

[32] About a month after these meetings, exactly on 20 February 1945, again in Rome, Arrigo Boldrini and other important members of the 28th Garibaldi Brigade were also received by Palmiro Togliatti, general secretary of the Communist Party and Vice President of the Council of Ministers of the Kingdom of Italy, who wanted to know the record of the partisan fighting unit in the context of the war conducted by the Allies.

German patrol spotted near "Casa di guardia", a position in the bend of the right bank of the Reno River from which it was possible to target Sant'Alberto, liberated by the 1st Canadian Infantry Division on 5 January. On 24 January, at dawn, the 9th Company neutralized a German sortie. By 8 February 1945 the total strength of the 28th Garibaldi Brigade amounted to 345 men. Each squad was equipped with 5 rifles, 4 automatic weapons, and a Bren machine gun. The headquarters Company had 4 automatic weapons and 2 rifles. Since the equipment was almost complete, it was necessary to quickly finish the weapon training.

Patrol activities continued without interruption, especially aimed at observing German movements. Efforts were then concentrated on the suppression of an enemy position in the Sant'Alberto area. The action began at 6:00 on 13 February with the support of mortars of the *"Cremona"* Combat Group. The position was not conquered but was isolated from the rest of the German forces. From 6:00 on 19 February 1945, the 28th Garibaldi Brigade was assigned to the *"Cremona"* Combat Group. The measure placed the section of the front line that went from the Canale di Bonifica to the Adriatic Sea under a single Italian command. At the same time, some men of the 44th Signal Company of the Italian Combat Group were attached to the *"Gordini"* Brigade to ensure communications with the headquarters[33].

On 23 February 1945 the Brigade's Medical Services were formed, under the responsibility of Professor Alfredo Badiali, former head of the civil hospital of Ravenna, assisted at the front by his son Carlo, a medical student, and by Remo Camerani (*Cupartòn*), previously responsible for the Medical Services of the *"Garavini"* Detachment. The plan for the conquest of Torre di Primaro (Ravenna), code name *"Rino"*, dates back to the last days of February 1945. The action aimed at strenghtening the right of the front held by the Allies along the Reno River. In this context, groups of *Garibaldini* were deployed in the direction of Chiavica Pedone, garrisoned by the enemy. During the night of 26 February, the 10th Company of the *"Gordini"* Brigade responded forcefully to the attack of several German patrols, repelling them. Operation *"Rino"* began on 1 March 1945. *Garibaldini* of the 10th Company supported the 3rd Company of the 1st Battalion of the 21st Infantry Regiment of the *"Cremona"* Group which, moving from Chiavica Scirocco, on the right bank of the Reno River, was to conquer Chiavica Pedone. The action was successful but the patriots suffered losses due to German mortar fire. An operation that the partisans were supposed to conduct with the use of boats in the lagoon of Comacchio was cancelled.

With the capture of Primaro, the 28th Garibaldi Brigade was entrusted with the defense of Chiavica Scirocco, a position almost impregnable but highly exposed to mortar and artillery fire. On 4 March, with the arrival on the line of the 12th Company, immediately assigned to the garrison of the western stronghold of Sant'Alberto, the formation led by *Bülow* reached a strength of 498 partisans. On 7 March General Charles Keightley, commander of the British V Corps, in which the *"Gordini"* Brigade had been placed, visited the partisan headquarters. Together with Boldrini, the high-ranking officer also inspected some positions on the Reno River and reviewed the 7th Company. The partisans were authorized to request the intervention of artillery and aerial reconnaissance for the operations to come. On 10 March, early in the morning, the 28th Garibaldi Brigade received another important visit, that of the Italian Prime Minister Ivanoe Bonomi, accompanied by the Minister of War Alessandro Casati and by General Clemente Primieri, commander of the *"Cremona"* Combat Group. On 13 March 1945 the *"Gordini"* Brigade would pass for a few days under the direct command of the 2nd Commandos Brigade[34], lined up from the Canale di Bonifica to the sea. At that time the 28th Garibaldi Brigade boasted a total strength of 580 men, of which 519 at the front and includ-

---

33 The decision to place the *"Gordini"* Brigade under the control of the *"Cremona"* Group meant that the relationship between partisans and the Italian soldiers intensified. The Combat Group included in its ranks former partisans of various political tendencies. Many of them were from Umbria, Marche and Tuscany regions.

34 Formerly 2nd Special Service Brigade, so renamed from 6 December 1944.

ed 15 partisan companies, 1 headquarters Company, 1 Medical Service and 1 Depot Company[35]. The enemy was going through a difficult moment but after a short period of calm marked by sporadic artillery duels, it had resumed harassing the Allied lines with patrol actions. The Germans also attempted to set up outposts on the right bank of the Reno River where they could set up camp at night to open fire on the positions held by the patriots. On 19 March 1945 the *"Gordini"* Brigade was once again assigned to the British V Corps. The completion of the personnel was followed by that of the equipment. In the space of a few days the *Garibaldini* received several means of transport that were added to the few available until then. On 22 March 1945 the Allies delivered 6 motorcycles for the headquarters and communication services. The number of boats, essential for carrying out amphibious operations, was increased[36].

According to what was reported by Arrigo Boldrini the motor pool included 8 heavy trucks, to which were added 2 more previously requisitioned, 5 Dodge light trucks, a truck used for communications, a water tank truck, a Jeep and 17 Triumph motorcycles. The equipment was completed by two Fiat 500 small cars, a Fiat 1500, a Fiat 1100, a workshop lorry, a car converted into an ambulance and several others motorcycles of an unspecified make. The use of trucks of Italian production Fiat 666 and Isotta Fraschini D65 is well documented. A rare photograph shows some vehicles used by the *"Gordini"* Brigade, among which Bedford OYD trucks (3 ton), probably obtained from the British, are recognisable. Another shot shows a captured German *Kübelwagen*. The vehicles were concentrated in a single unit essentially made up of drivers, the Transport Company, placed directly at the orders of the Brigade command. On 31 March other vehicles, probably some Jeeps, arrived. The portrait of Giuseppe Garibaldi on a white background, which corresponded to the vertical white pale of the Italian Tricolour, as a distinguishing sign, was to be painted on the vehicles of the Brigade[37]. The effigy of the Hero of Two Worlds was applied to the vehicles' front as evidenced by a photograph showing one of the Brigade Headquarters' Jeeps bearing the symbol in question on the lower left part of the windshield frame. The number of boats was also further expanded. These were maneuverable with oars, paddles and *paradelli*, long poles used to move boats in the waters of the Comacchio valleys. On 26 March General Keightley, commander of British V Corps, once again visited the *"Gordini"* Brigade, informing the partisan command of the unit's imminent employment in operations[38].

On 1 April 1945 at 22:00 the 2nd Commando Brigade, elements of the 9th Armoured Brigade and the 56th British Infantry Division moved forward to take the Smarlacca area, the Bellocchio coastal tower and the road that ran north from Po di Primaro[39] in order to secure a route towards Porto Garibaldi and Comacchio (province of Ferrara). The territory involved, sparsely populated and partially marshy, extended from the course of the Reno River to the Valletta Canal and was bordered to the east by the Adriatic coast and to the west by the Magnavacca Valley. The impossibility of using amphibious vehicles like the Fantails (name adopted to indicate the so-called Landing Vehicle Tracked also known as Buffalo) in shallow waters induced the Allies to request the most skilled rowers from

---

[35] The Depot Company was based in Ravenna and was responsible for administration, management of warehouses for various materials, recruitment of volunteers and their assignment to the Brigade's sub-units.

[36] The Allied commanders did not hide their concerns about the no man's land which separated the lines of the opposing armies and ranged from the left bank of the Reno River to Comacchio, patrolled by partisans with their boats. On the night of 25 March 1945, at "Ca' Nuova", on the left bank of the Reno River, *Garibaldini* from the 5th and 7th Companies captured 3 German soldiers who were wandering around. It was a stroke of luck because according to the partisan headquarters the area was not guarded by the enemy.

[37] The green and red vertical pales of the Italian Tricolour were represented by two stripes of smaller size than that of the white pale.

[38] Shortly after they were delivered additional PIAT grenade launchers which were issued to the 11th and 12th Companies.

[39] The place names Po di Primaro, Po di Volano, Po di Goro, Po di Gnocca and Po di Venezia identify branches of the Po River active at the time of the events narrated.

the 28th Garibaldi Brigade to maneuver the *battane* and other typical boats of the region, essential for the success of the operation. The companies of the partisan Brigade, generally divided into 3 squads, were then mainly formed by young volunteers.

Below are the names and years of birth of the commanders, deputy commanders and political commissioners of the Companies which formed the *"Gordini"* Brigade at the beginning of April 1945 (*Diario di Bulow*, op. cit.):

- Headquarters Company:
  - Commander Egidio Errani (1921);
  - Commissioner Ernesto Triossi (1904).

- 1st Company:
  - Commander Gaetano Trombini (1922);
  - Deputy Commander Enzo Foli (1919);
  - Commissioner Andrea Montanari (1914).

- 2nd Company:
  - Commander Alfonso Mainardi (1922);
  - Deputy Commander Mino Costa (1918);
  - Commissioner Gianni Bagnaresi (1923).

- 3rd Company:
  - Commander Ivo Zalambani (1925);
  - Deputy Commander Andrea Bonetti (1922);
  - Commissioner Mario Giacomoni (1924).

- 4th Company:
  - Commander Nino Beltrami (1912);
  - Deputy Commander Giovanni Zannoni (1921);
  - Commissioner Luigi Costa (1907).

- 5th Company:
  - Commander Ettore Servidei (1911);
  - Deputy Commander Balilla Ballotta (1911);
  - Commissioner Pietro Cesti (1919).

- 6th Company:
  - Commander Cristoforo Bendazzi (1924);
  - Deputy Commander Silvano Zaccaria (1920);
  - Commissioner Uno Errani (1916).

- 7th Company:
  - Commander Luciano Pezzi (1921);
  - Deputy Commander Francesco Gadoni (1915);
  - Commissioner Lino Bondi (1920).

- 8th Company:
  - Commander Francesco Guberti (1909);
  - Deputy Commander Delio Lombardi (1923);
  - Commissioner Elio Malta (1920).

- 9th Company:
  - Commander Alfredo Rafuzzi (1925);
  - Deputy Commander Mario Castelvetro (1921);
  - Commissioner Mario Fusconi (1919).

- 10th Company:
  - Commander Taschiero Casadio (1921);
  - Deputy Commander Teseo Tassinari (1922);
  - Commissioner Renato Dradi (1926).

- 11th Company:
  - Commander Giorgio Baffè (1923);
  - Deputy Commander Marino Zaccaria (1925);
  - Commissioner Virgilio Venturi (1900).

- 12th Company:
  - Commander Antonino Amadei (1921);
  - Deputy Commander Claudio Zaffagnini (1921);
  - Commissioner Carlo Mazzotti (1924).

- 13th Company:
  - Commander Dino Piccinini (1912);
  - Deputy Commander Vincenzo Tassinari (1924);
  - Commissioner Gino Monti (1916).

- 14th Company:
  - Commander Jules Minguzzi (1920);
  - Deputy Commander Domenico Schiavina (1913);
  - Commissioner Orano Angelini (1922).

- 15th Company:
  - Commander Ivan Miserocchi (1922);
  - Deputy Commander Edoardo Burrini (1923);
  - Commissioner Italo Vinci (1926).

- Transport Company:
  - Commander Antonio Morigi (1904);
  - Commissioner Arturo Minghelli (1907).

According to the agreement with the British commandos, the partisans of the 28th Garibaldi Brigade were supposed to occupy three buildings[40], Casone Agosta, Casone Le Fosse and Casone Naviglio

---

40 The term *Casone* identified a building which, in addition to hosting work activities and serving as accommodation,

all built on the Agosta embankment that separated the Mezzano Valley (located between Comacchio, Ostellato, Portomaggiore and Argenta) from the Fossa di Porto Valley (east of the Magnavacca Valley). On the night of 5 April 1945 at 3:00, after almost 6 hours of navigation in the darkness and in the open, the positions were reached and occupied. Boldrini and other members of the brigade headquarters, Captain Petre, British liaison officer to the partisan unit and another Allied officer took part in the action. In the following hours 3 strongholds were set up: 12 men with a radio apparatus for communications at Casone Agosta, the headquarters with 18 men at Casone Le Fosse, 5 men with signalling devices at Casone Naviglio. Patrol actions resulted in the capture of 14 German soldiers.

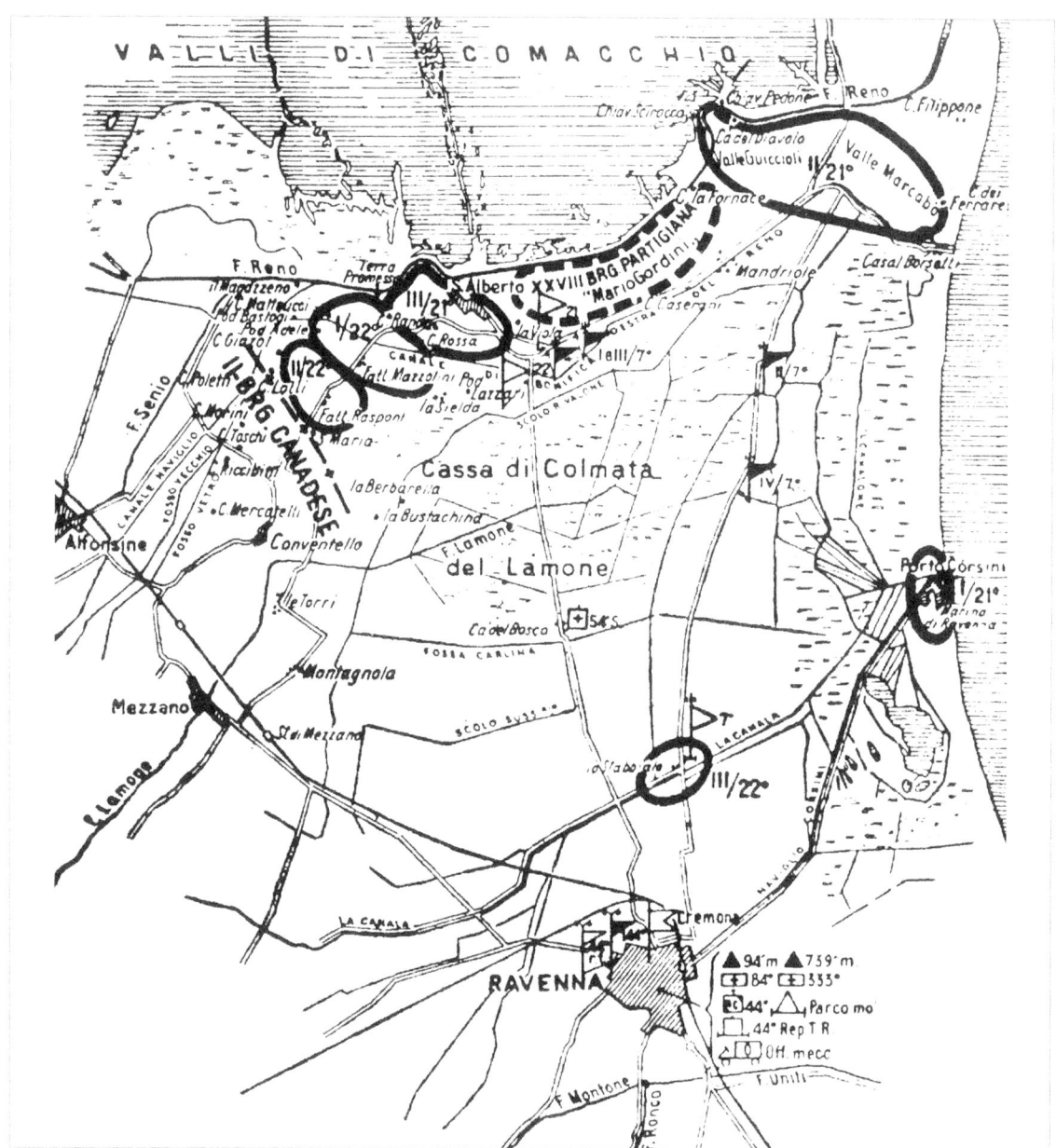

▲ Deployment at the front of the 28th Garibaldi Brigade on 23 January 1945.

was used as a post from which the valley guards operated to combat illegal fishing. The latter was the intended use of the *Casoni* Agosta, Le Fosse and Naviglio.

▲ Partisans of the *"Gordini"* Brigade maneuver a boat on the Reno River.

▼ Two partisans operate a Browning Cal. .50 machine gun. Po di Primaro, 24 February 1945.

▲ An image of Arrigo Boldrini in British uniform.

▲ General Clemente Primieri, commander of the *"Cremona"* Combat Group.

▲ Mortarmen of the *"Cremona"* Combat Group near Sant'Alberto. They wear typical British clothing and Mk II helmets.

▼ General Richard McCreery, commander of the British 8th Army.

▲ British generals McCreery and Keightley inspecting the 28th Garibaldi Brigade *"Mario Gordini"* during the ceremony to award the Gold Medal for Military Valor to Arrigo Boldrini. Ravenna, 4 February 1945.

▼ Partisans of the *"Gordini"* Brigade lined up in Piazza Garibaldi in Ravenna on 4 February 1945. The man in the foreground is armed with a Bren light machine gun, the girl in the background with a Sten submachine gun.

▲ General McCreery, commander of the British 8th Army, is about to decorate Boldrini. Behind him General Foulkes, commander of the Canadian I Corps (second from left) and General Primieri, commander of the *"Cremona"* Combat Group (fourth from left). Ravenna, 4 February 1945.

▼ Another picture of the high officials present at the ceremony to award the Gold Medal to Arrigo Boldrini.

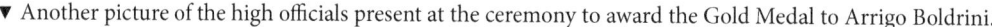

▲ Close-up of a young female partisan of the *"Gordini"* Brigade. This photograph was taken in Piazza Garibaldi in Ravenna on 4 February 1945.

▲ General Richard McCreery pins the Gold Medal for Military Valor to Arrigo Boldrini's chest.

▲ Arrigo Boldrini (*Bülow*) shows off the high military decoration he received.

▲ *Bülow* poses next to the flag of the *"Gordini"* Brigade after receiving the decoration.

▼ Four partisans armed with Lee Enfield No. 1 Mk IV rifles and a female partisan armed with a Sten submachine gun. These patriots of the *"Gordini"* Brigade were pictured in Ravenna on February 1945.

▲ Partisans of the 28th Garibaldi Brigade march singing through the streets of Ravenna. This photograph was taken on 4 February 1945.

▼ Men of the *"Gordini"* Brigade parading with the unit's flag in Ravenna, on the occasion of the commemoration of the massacre at Ponte dei Martiri, which took place on 25 August 1944. Twelve partisans lost their lives that day in retaliation.

▲ Arrigo Boldrini receives congratulations after being decorated with the Gold Medal for Military Valor.

▼ Another picture of partisans from the *"Gordini"* Brigade in Piazza Garibaldi in Ravenna. Some of them wear a red handkerchief around their necks.

▲ British General McCreery inspects the partisans of the 28th Garibaldi Brigade, followed by General Keightley and Arrigo Boldrini. Ravenna, 4 February 1945.

▼ Commemoration of the Fallen of the Ravenna Resistance. Among the names engraved on the tombstone stand out those of Umberto Ricci and Natalina Vacchi.

▲ Unloading the sheep which the partisans had shot on the far side of the Reno River. This picture dated from January 1945.

▼ The killed game is loaded by the partisans onto a cart. Reno River, January 1945.

▲ Partisans unload ammunition from a British 3-ton truck at the Brigade Headquarters.
▼ The headquarters of the *"Gordini"* Brigade near Sant'Alberto.

▲ Umberto II of Savoy visits the headquarters of the 28th Garibaldi Brigade, located in the Sant'Alberto area.

▼ For the supplies of the *"Gordini"* Brigade, horse-drawn vehicles were often adopted, such as the one in this photograph, used for transporting water.

▲ A partisan of the 8th Company, 28th Garibaldi Brigade. Affiliation to the sub-unit can be deduced from the number visible on the epaulette. The man is armed with a German-made *Maschinenpistole 40*. Vicinity of Sant'Alberto, 12 February 1945.

▲ The man in the previous photo look at two men busy freeing a Jeep from the mud. Surroundings of Sant'Alberto, 12 February 1945.

▼ Partisan of *"Mario Gordini"* Brigade armed with a Bren Mk I light machine gun. Mandriole (Ravenna), 28 February 1945.

▲ A very young partisan of *"Gordini"* Brigade poses sitting on the hood of a Jeep parked in front of the headquarters of the unit. Surroundings of Sant'Alberto, 24 February 1945.

▲ This picture shows Lucia Guerra who acted as secretary to Arrigo Boldrini. Before the war she was a student of philosophy at the university of Venice. After the Italian Armistice, she joined the Resistance, working on the spreading of propaganda and liaison between the partisans. Sant'Alberto, 29 March 1945.

▼ Infantrymen of the *"Cremona"* Combat Group escorting German prisoners. Casal Borsetti (Province of Ravenna), March 1945.

THE "MARIO GORDINI" BRIGADE TAKES PART IN THE FINAL ALLIED OFFENSIVE ON THE ITALIAN FRONT

On 6 April 1945 at 14:00, Marshal Alexander, Supreme Commander of the Allied Forces in Italy, visited the partisan headquarters. The Brigade's strength on the front line had grown further, numbering 547 men and 14 women. With Operation *Grapeshot*, the British 8th Army hoped to give the decisive push to the last German resistance south of the Po River. In the eastern section of the front, from the Ravenna-Ferrara road to the Adriatic coast, the 2nd Commandos Brigade, the 28th Garibaldi Brigade *"Mario Gordini"*, the British 9th Armoured Brigade and the 56th British Infantry Division, faced the German LXXVI Corps aligned from the Via Emilia (nowadays a modern highway called SS9) to the sea north of the Comacchio Valleys, comprising understrength units, more precisely the 162nd (*Turkmenen*) Infantry Division, the 42nd Jäger Division, the 362nd Infantry Division and the 98th Infantry Division. The *"Gordini"* Brigade was ordered to settle along the so-called spit of land between the Ussarola Valley and the Magnavacca Valley to the west, the Adriatic Sea to the east, the Podere Patrignani to the south, and the Valletta Canal to the north, replacing a British unit.

German troops and fascist republican units of the X Flottiglia MAS defended Porto Garibaldi to the north. The area was also littered with mines. The vast and marshy territory nevertheless allowed the partisans to hide the location of the strongholds from the enemy's view, thanks to the presence of widespread, though not dense, vegetation. At the 28th Garibaldi Brigade headquarters 2 doctors guaranteed the function of a Medical Service provided with 3 light British-made Humber FWD ambulances. A medical post was located near Mandriole. On 13 April 1945 the 4th battery of the 7th Artillery Regiment, commanded by Colonel Angelo Ottone, part of the *"Cremona"* Combat Group, was attached to the *"Gordini"* Brigade.

The first objectives assigned to the 4 25-pounder (88 mm) pieces of the Italian battery consisted of German positions that were targeting partisan positions with mortars and howitzers. In the following days patrols were mostly conducted under cover of darkness. Enemy fire remained sustained, there were machine gun nests in Porto Garibaldi and, in addition, numerous minefields made inaccessible the right bank of the Casal Borsetti canal port. To break the stasis on the front, the *"Gordini"* Brigade headquarters drew up a plan for a feint that would have invested the area between Canale Valletta and the town of Porto Garibaldi during the night. The 7th, 10th, 11th, 12th, 13th, and the 15th Companies would have been employed, acting as support units. The patrols would have been made up of 10 men with 2 automatic weapons and a pair of 2-inch (51 mm) British-made mortars. The action would have been preceded by intense artillery preparation, employing in a second phase illuminating rounds and smoke grenades. On 18 April, at 21:00, the Italian 25-pounders opened fire and immediately afterwards the *Garibaldini* launched their assault. The Germans, although reacting vigorously, suffered several losses. On the other hand, the partisans suffered 5 wounded, 3 from the 7th Company and 2 from the 13th Company. The raid ended in the middle of the night. On 20 April 1945 at 13:00, elements of the 7th, 8th, 10th, 11th, 12th and 15th Companies launched a second attack aimed at assessing the size of the enemy forces positioned on the Valletta Canal. The outcome was not the best and the partisans suffered losses that were far from negligible: 12 men wounded and 3 killed. The enemy was however about to retreat and so on 21 April the 1st and 6th Companies liberated Comacchio. At the same time, the 10th and 11th Companies mopped up Porto Garibaldi, while the 2nd, 3rd, 9th and 12th Companies proceeded to occupy the locality of San Giuseppe (Comacchio). During the night between 21 and 22 April 1945, the 28th Garibaldi Brigade was deployed as follows:

- the 9th Company was stationed at the little house beyond San Giuseppe while the 2nd, 3rd and 12th Companies were located in San Giuseppe, at "Casa Luogaccio";
- the 5th Company was at the villa positioned south of San Giuseppe, the 13th and 14th Companies were quartered at "Casa Scacchi" and at "Luogo Grande";
- the 7th Company was stationed at "Casa Belvedere"; the 10th and 11th Companies were located at "Villa Bellini" (Porto Garibaldi);
- the 1st and 6th Companies were stationed in Comacchio after having liberated the town;
- the headquarters, the headquarters Company, the drivers of the Transport Company, the men of the 4th, 8th and 15th Companies were instead at "Casa Vecchia" and "Casa Nuova", south of the Valletta Canal.

On 22 April, the partisan formation commanded by Arrigo Boldrini began a new advance. Almost all the companies concentrated in San Giuseppe with the vehicles, other elements of the Brigade continued to Lagosanto (province of Ferrara). On 23 April 1945 patrols of the *"Gordini"* Brigade took Pomposa (province of Ferrara) without a shot being fired. The 2nd, 3rd, 4th, 5th, 7th, 10th, 11th and 12th Companies reached the city and its immediate surroundings late in the evening. The crossing of the Po di Volano began at 18:00. The 8th, 9th, 13th, 14th and 15th Companies together with the headquarters and headquarters Company were stationed at Passo di Pomposa. The 1st and 6th Companies were camped in Codigoro (province of Ferrara). The British V Corps then ordered the 28th Garibaldi Brigade to pursue the retreating enemy and liberate Mesola (province of Ferrara), Loreo (province of Rovigo) and Chioggia (province of Venice). To better coordinate the advance, it was decided to form 4 columns, made up as follows:

- 1st column with 2nd, 3rd and 10th Companies;
- 2nd column with 4th, 5th and 12th Companies;
- 3rd column with 7th, 9th and 11th Companies;
- 4th column with 1st, 6th and 13th Companies.

The 8th, 14th and 15th Companies with the headquarters and various services remained available further behind. Overall, from 21 to 23 April 1945 the *"Gordini"* Brigade took 41 prisoners (22 Kalmyks enlisted in German units and 19 soldiers of the fascist National Republican Army). The partisan unit was once again placed at the orders of the *"Cremona"* Combat Group, operating on the right of the co-belligerent Italian formation. At that time the Brigade included 612 partisans and acted as a regular line infantry battalion. After quickly reaching Mesola on 24 April, the Po di Goro was crossed thanks to the use of improvised means. By 25 April 1945 the total number of enemy soldiers captured by the partisans at the orders of Arrigo Boldrini amounted to 268 men.

The Po River was reached and crossed near Taglio di Po (province of Rovigo), always with makeshift means. The 1st column was ordered to mop up the liberated area by carrying out reconnaissance in the direction of Polesella (province of Rovigo), the Po di Gnocca and the Po di Venezia. The 2nd column was tasked with liberating Contarina and Donada[41] and to subsequently settle on the Po di Levante[42], the 3rd column was to take Loreo. The enemy seemed to be completely in disarray and

---

[41] As of 1 January 1995, the Municipality of Contarina was merged with that of Donada to once again form the Municipality of Porto Viro, which was abolished on 10 February 1938.

[42] The Po di Levante was an ancient branch of the Delta of the River Po. Today it is the last section of the waterway Fissero-Tartaro-Canalbianco that connects Mantua to the Adriatic Sea.

during the march the partisans led by Boldrini repeatedly came across burnt vehicles, abandoned weapons, dead bodies and animal carcasses.

On 27 April, General Clemente Primieri, commander of the *"Cremona"* Combat Group ordered the *"Gordini"* Brigade to maintain contact with the routed enemy forces and to attempt to cross the Adige River. Crossing the river, which was in flood at the time, proved difficult and was only possible thanks to the help of the local population who, collaborating with the partisans, managed to set up improvised boats capable of supporting the weight of the vehicles. Chioggia and Sottomarina (province of Venice) were the final destinations of the 1st column while the 2nd and 4th columns had the task of stopping the retreat of the German garrison of Chioggia, a thousand men strong, gathering on the afternoon of 28 April along the right banks of the Brenta River and the Bacchiglione Torrent. The 3rd column was finally responsible for monitoring the area that extended from San Pietro di Cavarzere (province of Venice) to the Brentone Vecchio[43] (Chioggia) and deploying along the Brenta River. At 22:00 the Germans, through the local patriots, communicated that they wanted to surrender. Always helped by civilians, on 29 April 1945 the partisans of *"Gordini"* Brigade crossed the Brenta River. British commando units and Italian soldiers from the 22nd Infantry Regiment (*"Cremona"* Combat Group) also crossed the watercourse. According to what was agreed with General Zanussi, deputy commander of the *"Cremona"* Group, the 28th Garibaldi Brigade entered Codevigo (province of Padua) in the afternoon. The partisan unit camped in the town that represented the outlet on the lagoon of the province of Padua.

▲ Handshake between Arrigo Boldrini, commander of the 28th Garibaldi Brigade *"Mario Gordini"* and Lieutenant General Charles Keightley, commander of the British V Corps at the partisan headquarters on 7 March 1945.

---

43 Channel collecting and conveying runoff waters.

▲ Lieutenant General Charles Keightley talking to Arrigo Boldrini and partisans of the 7th Company during his visit to the headquarters of the 28th Garibaldi Brigade.

▼ Another picture showing General Charles Keightley with Arrigo Boldrini.

▲ Keightley and Boldrini inspect a *"Gordini"* Brigade forward lookout post on the Reno River.

▼ Arrigo Boldrini and Charles Keightley observe the front line and enemy positions from a forward lookout post along the Reno River.

▲ Prime Minister Ivanoe Bonomi and Minister of War Alfonso Casati visit the headquarters of the 28th Garibaldi Brigade. Arrigo Boldrini is on their left.

▼ A partisan of the *"Gordini"* Brigade explains the layout of positions to Ivanoe Bonomi.

▲ Prime Minister Bonomi poses with partisans of the 28th Garibaldi Brigade. One of them is a girl.

▼ Bonomi and Boldrini lead as the party sets out on a tour of *"Gordini"* Brigade units.

▲ This photograph shows from left to right Arrigo Boldrini (*Bülow*), Lieutenant Colonel Smuts of the British 8th Army, Edmondo Golinelli (*Libero*), commanding the 1st Battalion of the 36th Garibaldi Brigade *"Alessandro Bianconcini"* (a partisan unit) and Colonel of the Royal Italian Army Riccardo Esclapon di Villanova, head of the Military Intelligence Service to the British Army.

▼ Field Marshal Harold Alexander, commander of Allied forces in Italy, inspects a sub-unit of the 28th Garibaldi Brigade on 6 April 1945. Note the variety of weapons in the hands of the partisans: two German machine guns (MG 34s probably), Sten and Thompson submachine guns, a Lee Enfield No. 1 Mk IV rifle and a Beretta submachine gun.

▲ A rare picture of vehicles supplied to the 28th Garibaldi Brigade. Note three Bedford OYD trucks (3 tons). Codevigo (Povince of Padua), May 1945.

▼ The medical staff attached to the Brigade Headquarters, consisting of Italians and British personnel. In this picture you can recognize Carlo Badiali (third from left), Head of the Medical Service, medical captain Wean (fourth from left) and Remo Camerani (fifth from left), Head of the Medical Service at the front. Behind them two light ambulances Humber FWD are visible. Pomposa (province of Ferrara), April 1945.

▲ Another photograph, taken in Pomposa (province of Ferrara) at the end of April 1945, depicting members of the Brigade Medical Service.

END OF OPERATIONS AND DISBANDMENT OF THE BRIGADE

With the conclusion of the military operations, an opinion was forwarded to the Allies regarding the demobilization of the formation: the ceremony would be celebrated in Ravenna in the presence of a high representative of the Corpo Volontari della Libertà (organization on which the Brigade depended) and of the Minister of occupied Italy Mauro Scoccimarro. The partisans would receive a cash prize and a certificate issued by the British 8th Army and the war flag of the *"Gordini"* Brigade would be proposed for an Italian military honor[44].

Among the requests made was also that regarding the granting of concrete aid to the families of fallen and wounded patriots[45]. Boldrini recalls that in the Codevigo area the relations with some religious authorities have not proved optimal due to an active propaganda against the resistance aimed at inducing the population not to get acquainted with the partisans.

More worrying was the persecution carried out against the soldiers of the Italian Social Republic and the civilians of fascist orientation after the end of hostilities[46]. The commander of the 28th Garibaldi Brigade expressed the impossibility to suppress this phenomenon, identifying the triggering cause in the ferocious Nazi-Fascist conduct during the years of occupation. The command of the *"Gordini"*[47] Brigade, according to Boldrini, could not but recommend his men self-discipline, counting on the collaboration of other partisan formations operating in the region, with a view to full political and moral responsibility. The enormous tensions, arising from that climate of settling of scores which is the tragic consequence of every conflict characterised by fratricidal clashes, were also exacerbated by strictly personal events that led to real revenge.

The executions that took place from late April to late June 1945, a period certainly longer than that of the *"Gordini"*'s stay on site, caused 136 victims. It is important to point out that the area where the massacres took place would not be limited to Codevigo and its surroundings. The killings of fascist civilians and soldiers considered responsible for very serious repressive actions against populations and patriots, would have been committed by elements of various origins and not only by those fighters who operated autonomously and contrary to the directives issued by military chiefs of the *"Cremona"* Combat Group and the 28th Garibaldi Brigade[48].

---

44 The Ravenna partisan brigade *"Mario Gordini"* will in fact be awarded the Silver Medal for Military Valor. This is the motivation: *"First in the clandestine struggle, then under the command of allied units, and finally alongside and in close collaboration with a large unit of our renewed army, inspired by the purest traditions of the Risorgimento and Garibaldi's volunteerism, it fought against the traditional enemy, the Germans, and won for the freedom and reconstruction of Italy."* Ravenna - Comacchio Marshes - Brenta River, 15 September 1943 - 30 April 1945.

45 Overall, the 28th Garibaldi Brigade *"Mario Gordini"* suffered 187 losses (one of the most reliable estimates cites 44 dead and 143 wounded).

46 Arrigo Boldrini, *Diario di Bulow*, op. cit., p. 280.

47 At the end of the operations the command of the *"Gordini"* Brigade was composed as follows:
- Brigade Commander: Arrigo Boldrini
- Deputy Brigade Commanders: Ateo Minghelli and Mario Verlicchi
- Chief of Staff: Pellegrino Montanari
- Political Commissioners: Gino Gatta and Ennio Cervellati
- Deputy Political Commissioner: Tino Ghiselli
- Head of the Medical Service at the front: Remo Camerani
- Head of the Medical Service: Carlo Badiali.

48 The Court of Padua dealt with the events of Codevigo in numerous proceedings. Four partisans of the 28th Garibaldi Brigade were also tried and acquitted. No criminal proceedings were ever brought against the heads of the *"Gordini"* Brigade and the *"Cremona"* Group because the events took place against the orders issued by them and without their knowledge.

Among those who were taken and executed were individuals from the province of Ravenna. This led to the assumption that the perpetrators of the massacres came from the same areas as their victims. Regardless of their actual affiliation, the executioners would therefore have acted by deduction or direct knowledge.

The topic, certainly difficult, is still a source of bitter debate. This is a matter that can be approached with extreme caution, since in such cases the search for truth is often susceptible to being hindered by partial knowledge of events, by political prejudices and the consequent temptation to instrumentalise facts, in one way or another.

On 15 May 1945 a meeting between Italian officers and the leaders of the *"Gordini"* Brigade, which was also attended by Umberto of Savoy, was held in Adria (province of Rovigo), at the headquarters of the *"Cremona"* Combat Group. The Lieutenant of the Realm urged the partisan commanders to express their opinions regarding the role played by the Italian monarchy in the War of Liberation, an invitation that was accepted with extreme frankness.

Arrigo Boldrini states: *"So, the Cremona Combat Group headquarters was in Adria. General Primieri organized a lunch with the crown prince and also invited us from the 28th Brigade. We arrived a little late from the front, we had a jeep that was not working well. I happened to sit right in front of Umberto, and at the table this very nice and cordial conversation began. And at a certain point Umberto of Savoy told me «But what would you have done in my place on 8 September?». I answered immediately: «Your Majesty, I would have parachuted into the North». And he answered calmly, lowering his voice a little: «You know, my father didn't want it.». Almost a confession. Can you imagine, the monarchist generals Primieri and Zanussi! They looked at me with hatred! Incredible! Because having told them that thing had made Umberto feel sad. Then I understood that they were upset by the King's response, who could have said perhaps «The Allies did not want», a political reason in short, instead he told the truth, that it was his father. And thank goodness! Imagine if he had been sent to the North to join the Resistance! Maybe the monarchy wouldn't even have fallen!"*[49].

In Piove di Sacco (Province of Padua) on 16 May 1945 at 9:00, patriots of the 28th Garibaldi Brigade and soldiers from the 21st Infantry Regiment were preparing to be reviewed by Umberto II of Savoy and by Allied and Italian high-ranking officers who had some fears, perhaps excessive, for the safety of the Lieutenant of the Realm: the partisans could have been hostile, since they were against the monarchy. Upon the arrival of the heir to the throne, as soon as the notes of the Royal March (*Marcia Reale*) sounded, insults and whistles of disapproval broke out. From one part of the troops lined up, an anti-monarchist song could be heard being sung loudly, *"The House of Savoy is already trembling"* (*Già trema la Casa Savoia*)[50]. The bedlam erupted, British and Italian officers tried to protect Umberto but nothing happened. The vigorous protests had been vibrated by infantrymen of the *"Cremona"* Group. The partisans of the *"Gordini"* Brigade, on the other hand, carried out the orders given to perfection and presented their weapons impeccably.

The insubordination of Italian soldiers, among whose ranks, it should be remembered, there were many former partisans, was not triggered in any way by political representatives of the Garibaldi Brigade. Boldrini and his comrades understood that Umberto's visit had no ill-concealed propaganda intentions but could, on the contrary, have represented an extraordinary opportunity to express due recognition of the efforts made by Italian soldiers of the Royal Army and partisans, to liberate the country. The decision on the official date for the disbandment of the formation led by *Bülow* was definitively taken in the days immediately following the visit of the prince. The vehicles supplied to

---

49 Cesare De Simone, *Gli anni di Bulow*, Mursia, Milano 1996.

50 This song, perhaps better known by the title *"Death to the House of Savoy"* (*A morte la Casa Savoia*), goes in one of its most popular versions as follows: *"Death to the House of Savoy / Bathed in the shame of blood / The languishing people awaken / The languishing people awaken / O thieves of our sweat / In the world we are all brothers / We are the rebellious ranks / Let us arise because the end has come / Death to the King and the little prince! / Death to the King and little prince!"*

the partisans, including the Jeeps, received as a gift by Boldrini from the higher commands, were destined for the organization of a road haulage cooperative. The weapons were delivered to the depots indicated by the Allies and the demobilization of the 28th Garibaldi Brigade *"Mario Gordini"* was celebrated in Piazza Marconi in Ravenna, on 20 May 1945.

▲ The 7th Company of the *"Gordini"* Brigade.

▲ *Garibaldini* from the 8th Company of the *"Gordini"* Brigade. There is a fair amount of variety in clothing, many wear summer clothes but almost all wear the British *"General Service Cap"* complete with Italian tricolour cockade.

▼ The 14th Company of the 28th Garibaldi Brigade. The men are wearing typical British uniforms.

▲ Members of 10th Company, *"Mario Gordini"* Brigade. The second partisan standing from the right wears a German belt.

▼ Partisans of the *"Gordini"* Garibaldi Brigade. The number of women enlisted in the unit grew with time.

▲ Elements of the 8th Company, 28th Garibaldi Brigade.

▼ The 13th Company of the *"Gordini"* Brigade.

▲ The 6th Company portrayed in Codevigo (Province of Padua) in May 1945. On the right, standing, wearing shorts, the commander Silvano Zaccaria who had replaced Cristoforo Bendazzi, drowned in the Brenta River while trying to rescue some British soldiers on 28 April 1945.

▼ Partisans belonging to the 10th Company of the *"Gordini"* Brigade.

▲ Gino Gatta, Arrigo Boldrini and Ennio Cervellati portrayed on the balcony of a building in Conselice (Province of Ravenna) on 17 April 1945.

▲ Another shot depicting Gatta, Boldrini and Cervellati in Conselice.

▲ On the right in this photograph, Cristoforo Bendazzi, former commander of the 6th Company. On the left, the partisan Enzo Pasi.

▼ Arrigo Boldrini gives a speech in Conselice on 17 April 1945. With him are Ennio Cervellati and three female partisan couriers.

▲ A FIAT 666 truck of the *"Gordini"* Brigade loaded with partisans. The unit sign painted on the front left of the cab is something to note.

▼ Motorcyclists of the 28th Garibaldi Brigade.

▲ Motorcycles and motor vehicles used by the *"Gordini"* Brigade. Note, at the center of the photograph, the presence of a captured German *Kübelwagen*.

▼ Trucks of the *"Gordini"* Brigade. A big star has been fixed on the front of the truck in the foreground.

▲ The motorized column of the 28th Garibaldi Brigade, led by a Jeep, moving in Ravenna on 20 May 1945.

▼ A motorcyclist of the *"Gordini"* Brigade. The motorcycle is probably a Triumph 3HW. Ravenna, 20 May 1945.

▲ Two partisans of the 28th Garibaldi Brigade riding their motorcycles immortalized on the day of the demobilization of the unit. The one on the right is Pietro Cesti, former fighter pilot in the Royal Italian Air Force, political commissioner of the 5th Company.

▼ Partisans and civil authorities on the balcony of the municipal building of Ravenna.

▲ The banquet organized on the occasion of the demobilization of the *"Gordini"* Brigade. Ravenna, 20 May 1945.

▲ Two patriots from the *"Mario Gordini"* Garibaldi Brigade take part in the banquet organized by the Italian Women's Union (Unione Donne Italiane). Ravenna, 20 May 1945.

▲ A partisan equipped with a Bren machine gun portrayed on the day of the demobilization of the Brigade in Ravenna.

▼ Umberto of Savoy meets the population in Codevigo.

▲ Parade of partisans of the 28th Garibaldi Brigade in Ravenna. The second man from the left is Alberto Bardi (*Falco*), commander of the unit from June to December 1944.

▼ The partisan depicted on the left in the foreground is Mario Giacomoni (*Portos*), political commissar of the 3rd Company. Ravenna, 20 May 1945.

▲ Isotta Fraschini D65 truck of the 28th Garibaldi Brigade. The unit sign, consisting of the effigy of Giuseppe Garibaldi on a white background between two vertical stripes, one green, the other red, is painted on the vehicle front.

▲ *Garibaldini* portrayed in Ravenna during the demobilization ceremony of the Brigade.

▼ A group of partisans from the 28th Garibaldi Brigade in Ravenna on 20 May 1945.

▲ Flag bearer of the 28th Garibaldi Brigade *"Mario Gordini"*. On 4 November 1945 the Silver Medal of Military Valor was awarded to the *"Gordini"* Brigade flag and this photo was taken in Turin to commemorate it.

▲ The last parade of the 28th Garibaldi Brigade in Ravenna. The partisans march in their British battledresses.

▼ From left to right on this Jeep of *"Gordini"* Brigade, you can recognize important members of the Brigade headquarters: the political commissar Gino Gatta (*Zalet*), the deputy political commissioner Ennio Cervellati (*Silvio*) and Florio Rossi (*Galvani*), head of the intelligence service. Arrigo Boldrini is sitting next to the driver. On the lower left part of the windshield frame of the vehicle, the effigy of Garibaldi is visible on a light background.

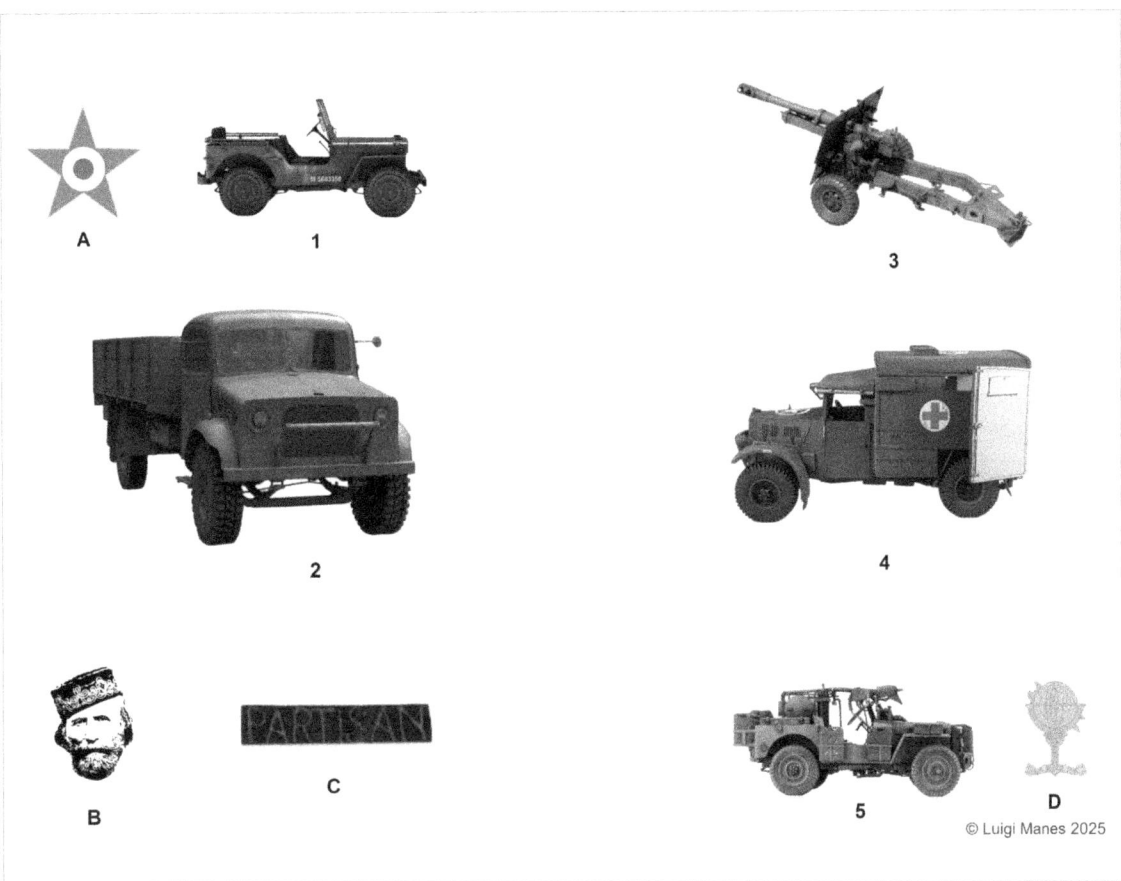

A: Partisan badge consisting of a tricolour star bordered in yellow adopted by Garibaldi's formations.
B: Portrait of Giuseppe Garibaldi applied to the front of some vehicles of the *"Gordini"* Brigade.
C: Shoulder patch for British uniforms issued to the 28th Garibaldi Brigade.
D: Popski's Private Army cap badge. Sometimes, reproduced in a stylised manner, it was also present on the unit's vehicles.

1: Jeep used by the General Staff of the 28th Garibaldi Brigade. The last two digits of the War Department number are fictitious.
2: Bedford OYD lorry (3 ton) used by the 28th Garibaldi Brigade.
3: British 25-pounder gun. Artilleries of this type armed four of the six groups which formed the 7th Artillery Regiment included in the *"Cremona"* Combat Group.
4: Humber FWD light ambulance supplied to the medical unit at the *"Gordini"* Brigade Headquarters in April 1945.
5: Jeep equipped with Wasp Mk II flamethrower tested in Italy by Popski's Private Army.

BIBLIOGRAPHY

- Battaglia Roberto, *"Storia della Resistenza Italiana"*, Einaudi, Torino, 1953.
- Bocca Giorgio, *"Storia dell'Italia Partigiana - Settembre 1943 – Maggio 1945"*, Mondadori, Milano, 1995.
- Boldrini Arrigo *"Diario di Bulow - Pagine di lotta partigiana 1943 – 1945"*, Vangelista, Milano, 1985.
- Casadio Gianfranco e Cantarelli Rossella, *"La Resistenza nel Ravennate"*, Edizioni Del Girasole, Ravenna, 1980.
- Crippa Paolo e Luigi Manes, *"I Mezzi delle Unità Cobelligeranti"*, Mattioli 1885, Fidenza (PR), 2018.
- De Simone Cesare, *"Gli Anni di Bulow"*, Mursia, Milano, 1996.
- Giadresco Gianni, *"Guerra in Romagna 1943 – 1945"*, Il Monogramma, Ravenna, 2004.
- Giadresco Gianni, *"La Battaglia di Ravenna"*, Editori Riuniti, Roma, 1964.
- Klinkhammer Lutz, *"L'Occupazione Tedesca in Italia - 1944 – 45"*, Bollati Boringhieri, Torino, 1993.
- Masetti Giuseppe e Antonio Panaino (a cura di), *"Parola d'ordine Teodora"*, Longo, Ravenna, 2005.
- Meluschi Antonio (a cura di), *"Epopea Partigiana"*, SPER, Bologna, 1947.
- Montali Edmondo, *"Il Comandante Bulow - Arrigo Boldrini partigiano, politico, parlamentare"*, Futura Editrice, Roma, 2016.
- Nozzoli Guido, *"Quelli di Bulow - Cronache della 28ª Brigata Garibaldi"*, Editori Riuniti, Roma, 1957.
- Peniakoff Wladimir, *"Corsari in Jeep"*, Garzanti, Milano, 1951.
- Rendina Massimo, *"Italia 1943/1945 - Guerra Civile o Resistenza?"*, Newton & Compton, Roma, 1994.

TITOLI GIÀ PUBBLICATI - TITLES ALREADY PUBLISHING

BOOKS TO COLLECT

www.ingramcontent.com/pod-product-compliance
Ingram Content Group UK Ltd.
Pitfield, Milton Keynes, MK11 3LW, UK
UKHW060213240426
12048UKWH00031BB/1712

9 791255 892373